KT-487-538

AN ANCIENT CAPITAL OF
MANY SPLENDOURS

XI'AN

Edited by The Foreign Affairs Office Of Xian Municipal Government
Published by China Tourism Press

A Chronological Table of Xi'an and Concurrent Events in a Number of Ancient Civilizations in the World

	1,500,000 BC	5000 BC	3000 BC	1500 BC	700 BC
Xi'an	(**c. 1. 15 million years ago**) Lantian Man lived at the northern side of the Qinling Mountains.	(**Approximately 5,000 years ago**) Banpo Man settled by the shore of the Chan River and created the Painted Pottery Culture. During the late Neolithic age, Huang Di (Yellow Emperor) and Yan Di lived in the Yellow River basin.		(**1136 BC**) King Wen of Zhou established his capital on the west bank of the Feng River; (**1133 BC**) King Wu of Zhou established his capital on the east bank of the Feng River.	The state of Qin moved its capi from Yueyang to Xiangyang.
	 A sculpture of Lantian Man.	Painted pottery basin. 	 Yellow Emperor's Mausoleum at Xuanyuan	A Western-Zhou Bronze Tripod. 	A tiger-shaped tally of th Qin. 
Egypt	The Palaeolithic age.	(**4241 BC**) Appearance of the first calendar; (**3100-2685 BC**) The Archaic Period.	(**2685-2180 BC**) The Ancient Empire; (**2133-1786 BC**) The Middle Empire.		(**670-651 BC**) Rule of the Assyria (**525 BC**) Conquered by Persia; (**304-30 BC**) Reign of the Ptolem Empire.
India		(**4000-3000 BC**) The Stone Age.	(**c. 2750 BC**) The birth of Indian Civilization in the Indus Valley; The invading Aryan troops conquered the Indus and Ganges river valleys.		(**566 BC**) The birth of Sakyamuni
Persia		The Neolithic age.			(**558 BC**) Cyrus II annexed the va ous tribes and established the Pers Empire.
Greece	(**6,500 years ago**) The advent of agriculture.	(**3000 BC**) A settled life began.	(**1600-1100 BC**) Heyday of the Mycenaean Culture.	(**c. 1200 BC**) The Hellenic Age in which Homer lived. (**1000-5000 BC**) Greek's colonies kept expanding and the city of Athens was founded and prospered.	
Rome			(**735 BC**) Founding of Rome.	(**753-509 BC**) Reign of seven kings; (**509-27 BC**) The Republic age.	

300 **BC**	150 **BC**	**AD**	200 **AD**	350 **AD**
(221 BC) The state of Qin conquered six rival states and founded a centralized monarch; **(206 BC)** Liu Bang made himself emperor of the Western Zhou Dynasty and established his capital in Chang'an.	**(138 BC)** On a diplomatic mission to West Territory, Zhang Qian pened up the Silk Road; China invented paper-making technology during the Western Han Dynasty.	Dong Zhuo wreaked havoc and abducted Emperor Xian of Han to Chang'an.	**(319 AD)** Liu Yao moved his capital to Chang'an and founded the Early Zhao Dynasty; **(384-417 AD)** Shi Le, a leader of the Pingjie nomads, founded the Late Zhao Dynasty.	**(351-394 AD)** Fu Jian, a tribal leader, established the Early Qin Dynasty; **(557-581 AD)** Yao Chang, a Qiang leader, established the Late Qin Dynasty.
Terracotta archer in the standing position. A Han-dynasty decorative tile-end wit decorative tiger patterns.  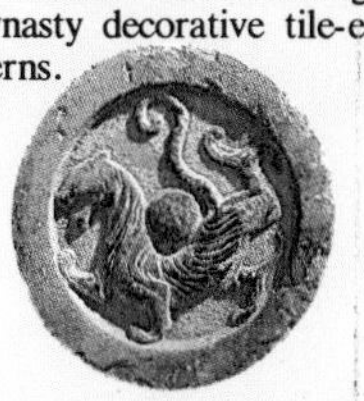		"A Horse Resting Its Hoofs on a Xiongnu Enemy", stone sculpture in front of Huo Qubing's tomb. A stone animal. 	 The pottery sculpture of a mounted horn-tooting figurine.	 The pottery sculpture of an armoured horse and warrior.
(304-30 BC) Role of the Ptolemaic Empire; **(168 BC)** Became a dependency to Rome.	**(30 BC)** Egypt became a Roman province.	**(30BC-615AD)** Under the rule of the Roman Empire.		
Reign of the Maurya Empire.	(Second century BC-first century AD) The Greeks invaded and ruled North India.			**(401 AD)** Fa Xian, a high monk from China, arrived in India.
(323-170 BC) Rule of successors of Alexander the Great; **(170 BC)** Parthia declared independence and formed an empire.		Reign of the Parthian Empire.	**(337-371 AD)** In war with the Roman Empire.	**(337-371 AD)** In war with the Roman Empire.
	(146 BC) Greece came under the Roman rule.			
Rise of Macedon, and Alexander the Great launched an expedition.	**(73 BC)** Spartacus rose in an armed uprising; **(27 BC)** Beginning of the Roman Empire.	**(64 AD)** Rome was burned to ground.	**(395 AD)** Split into east and west empires; **(476 AD)** Demise of Western Roman Empire.	**(395 AD)** The Roman Empire split into Eastern and Western Empires; **(476 AD)** The Demise of the west Roma Engine.

500 **AD**	580 **AD**	600 **AD**	650 **AD**	1300 **AD**	1400 **AD**
(535-557 AD) Yu Wentai founded the Western Wei Dynasty; **(557-581 AD)** Yu Wenyong established the Northern Zhou Dynasty.	**(581 AD)** The Sui Dynasty reunified China; **(582 AD)** Construction of the city of Daxing commenced.	**(618 AD)** Li Yuan established the Tang Dynasty, ascended to the throne and founded his capital in Chang'an; the Silk Road came into its own once again. **(629 AD)** Xuan Zang left Chang'an on a pilgrimage to India.	**(713AD)** The Tang Dynasty enjoyed unprecedented prosperity during the Kaiyuan Reign, and a number of celebrated poets, including Li Bai and Du Fu, came to the fore during; **(c. 730 AD)** The invention of the printing technology. **(904 AD)** Zhu Wen destructed the capital city of Chang'an.	**(1374 AD)** Construction of the Ming-dynasty Chang'an came under way.	
	 A statue of Dong Qin.	A tri-colour glazed pottery of a galloping horse. 	 A cup of woven gold filigree.	Ming-dynasty Chang'an. 	
Under the rule of the Eastern Roman empire.				**(1517-1880 AD)** Under the rule of the Ottoman Empire.	
(570 AD) Demise of the Gupta Dynasty.		**(606 AD)** Founding of the Harsha Dynasty	**(1206-1526 AD)** The Delhi Sultanate controlled most of the Hindu states.		**(1526 AD)** Founding of the Mogul Empire.
(531-579 AD) The heyday of the Sassanid Dynasty.	**(589 AD)** Came under the attack of the Arabs.	**(651 AD)** The Sassanid Dynasty fell to the Arabs. (Latter half of the sixth century AD) Came under the control of the Byzantine Empire.	**(1256 AD)** The Mongols subjugated the entire Persia.		**(1520 AD)** A new Persian Empire was born.
(C. 500 AD) Part of Greece came under the control of Persia			Came under the rule of the Byzantine Empire.		Greece came under Turkish control.
		(617-673 AD) Constantinople under the threat of the Persians and the Arabs.			**(1453AD)** Constantinople sacked by the Ottoman army; the perish of the Byzantine Empire.

Contents

INTRODUCTION

Prompted by the venerated history of China as one of the world's four earliest civilizations, a philosopher of the ancient times mused aloud that all those seeking the truth should go to China. Taking the hint, a contemporary philosopher added that no visit to China is complete without a journey to Xi'an. This line reflects, to certain extents, the important position Xi'an holds as a famed historical and cultural city and one of China's six major ancient capitals.

Indeed, Xi'an has made unparalleled contributions to the history and traditional culture of China. For more than one millennium, it had been the stage on which the histories of a dozen or so Chinese dynasties unfolded. Every move and every action that originated in this city could have far-reaching influence on the course of China's social development. It is where Zhou-dynasty aristocrats instituted rites and composed music while making libations to gods and ancestors and feasting themselves out of bronze utensils, and where they inscribed their laws in bronzeware and stone tablets, many of which were to remain to this day. It is where the Qin army launched eastern expeditions, eliminated six rival states and initiated a centralized autocracy whose principles would endure for more than a hundred generations to come. It is where Han and Tang monarchs established their capital city of Chang'an, which was the eastern terminus of the celebrated Silk Road and an oriental metropolis thronged with visitors and merchants from every nook and corner of the world.

The rich and deep-rooted historical and cultural heritage of Xi'an is vindicated by a wealth of cultural relics and historical sites that pockmark its land. The city roads may have been leisurely promenaded by emperors more than a thousand years ago; the rippling verdure on the outskirts is strewn with tombs of deceased emperors, empresses, aristocrats, ranking officials or men of letters. Pick up a fragment of something from the ground, and it may turn out to be part of a Qin-dynasty brick, a Han-dynasty tile or a Tang-dynasty porcelainware. Dig into the field, and probably you will be pleasantly surprised by the emergence of a terracotta warrior which has lain there for ages.

In English this country is called "China", which is actually the transliteration of the ideogram which means "Qin". Those live in Xi'an and its vicinity are direct descendents of the Qin people. Emperors of the remote antiquity chose Xi'an as their capital partly because of its fertile land and sufficient water supply and partly because the place was made militarily formidable by the range upon range of mountains that skirted it. It is precisely because of the secluded location that Xi'an was able to preserve its adorable history and culture to this day. The local dialect of Xi'an and the Guanzhong Plain is redolent of the rhythm and timbre of archaic Chinese, and local diet and residences evince an air of venerable age and sanctity. Weddings, funerals, celebrations and social etiquette are in many ways evocative of the social mores and traditions of bygone dynasties of Zhou, Qin, Han and Tang.

Xi'an may be a shade less glamourous and sophisticated than many of its counterparts in today's world, but it is catching up rapidly thanks to the policy of reform and opening up to the outside world. By carrying forward the enterprising spirit of the forefathers of the Zhou and Qin ages and inheriting the openness and magnanimity of the Han and Tang dynasties, the ancient city of Xi'an is transforming itself into a modern metropolis with an impressive setup of commerce, trade, tourism, science and technology and education. Xi'an today is striving to rejuvenate the glory of Han and Tang days, reopen the Silk Road to the world today, and emerge once again as a booming international town. Xi'an, an old city with a glorious yesterday, certainly will have a very promising tomorrow.

图1　黄河龙门

1. The Dragon on the Yellow River.

Life and Creations of the Ancestors

Xi'an, a city steeped in history and fable, nestles in the central Wei River valley on the western shore of the Yellow River. The valley, known poetically as the 800-li Qin Plain, is endowed with a vast expanse of fertile farmland and an abundance of natural resources; it is also home to countless great men of past times who have filled history with their deeds and the land with their renown. With its sublime culture matched by a landscape of verdant mountains and sparkling waters, Xi'an is a glistening gem imbedded in the Loess Plateau.

On the southern edge of Xi'an rises the Qinling Mountains, a hundred-mile chain of lofty peaks which is only part of a natural screen encompassing the statuesque Mount Huashan, known as the Western Mountain Sanctuary of Chinese Buddhism, the Lishan Mountain in Lintong, famous for its hot springs, the Zhongnanshan Mountain, its trove of natural treasures cocooned under rich verdure, and the Taibai Mountain, mystified by a perpetual mantle of snow. A labyrinth of waterways — the Wei, Jing, Chan, Ba, Feng, Hao, Yu and Lao rivers — encircles the city like eight glistening silk ribbons.

The strategic importance of Xi'an between the Qinling Mountains and the Wei River is enhanced by Tongguan Pass to the east and Sanguan Pass to the west. In the north a hundred-metre-wide road was paved during the Qin Dynasty to replenish provisions a thousand li away for soldiers fighting the Xiongnu nomads in Inner Mongolia. In the south, the Meridian Road and the Tangluo, Baoxie and Chencang trails conduct to the ancient states of Ba and Shu by way of the Hanzhong Plain. In the southeast, the Wuguan Trail cuts through the Shangluo Mountain to provide vital access to the former turf of Chu. This extensive land-and-water transportation network, coupled with a strategic location which is a boon to defenders and a bane to attackers, explains why in bygone years so many monarchs chose Xi'an as their dream site for a capital.

Archaeological surveys show that this is the site of many ruins of the Palaeolithic and Neolithic ages, most of which are scattered about the shores of the Wei River. In 1964, fossils of Lantian Man were discovered at Gongwangling, Lantian County; in 1978, fossils of Dali Man who lived 200,000 years ago were brought to light along with the remains of Luonan, Changwu and Huanglong men. All these archaeological finds indicate that long before mankind had crossed the threshold of civilization, the Xi'an area was already teeming with human activity. Massive ruins uncovered at Bantang in Xi'an, Jiangzhai in Lintong, and Beishouling in Baoji are attributed to the Yangshao Culture which was typical of the Neolithic age in the Yellow River basin. These historical sites with a wealth of cultural relics stand as fitting epitaphs to the superlative wisdom and splendid cultural attainments of our ancestors who lived five to six millennia ago.

West Guanzhong Plain and the Loess Plateau north of the Wei River were where Yan Di and Huang Di (Yellow Emperor), forefathers of the Chinese nation, lived with their tribes. It was these two legendary leaders that wrote finale to the age of barbarity in which man subsisted on raw animal meat and wild fruit, and turned the Loess Plateau into the cradle for a nation to emerge and create an immortal civilization. Yellow Emperor's Mausoleum at Qiaoshan, Huangling County, and Yan Di's Mausoleum in the suburbs of Baoji, are meccas for those Chinese who feel obliged to go the extra mile to pay homage to these two sages and owe what they are today to them.

8. A fossil of the skullcap of Lantian Man exhumed in May 1964; archaeological studies reveal that this skull belonged to a middle-aged female.
9. The foot of the Qinling Mountains, where Lantian Man lived and propagated.

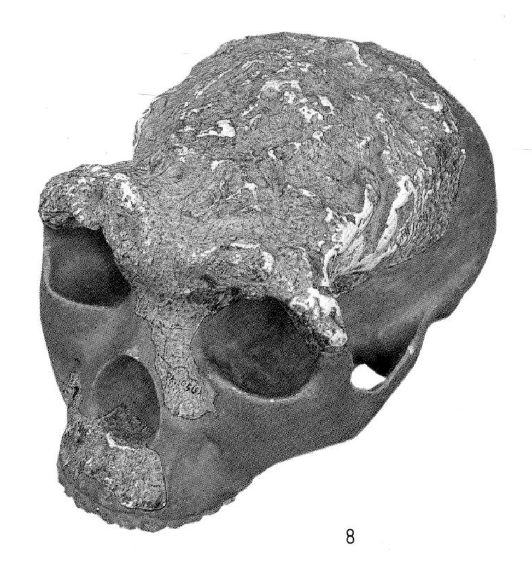
8

9

Banpo: From Benightment to Civi-lization

10. A protective shelter has been built to protect the ruins of primitive abodes discovered at Banpo Village and accommodate visitors from all over the world.
11. An ornament with human-mask and fish designs. ▶
12. This pottery basin with human-mask and fish designs, 40 cm in diameter and 17 cm in height, is representative of Banpo Man's painted pottery; the natural simplicity of the designs painted on the interior of the basin reflects Banpo Man's distinct aesthetic taste.

Banpo, a village situated by the Chan River on the eastern outskirts of Xi'an, is the site of a large tribe living in the Yellow River basin during the Neolithic age. The ruins, which cover a total area of 50,000 square metres, were discovered in 1953, and full-scale excavation began a year later under the auspices of the Archaeology Institute of the Chinese Academy of Sciences. The 10, 000-square-metre site now on display is merely the tip of an iceberg.

The ruins are scattered about a roughly circular domain skirted by a moat five metres deep and five metres wide. An ditch divided the place in two, indicating that probably two tribes had lived in this place. Each section had a large public house surrounded by smaller ones with doors opened in its direction. Some of the abodes were built on the ground, and the others were dug half way underground; most abodes were round and only a few were square. Houses built on the ground had wooden roofs, and their walls were made of thin wooden sticks tightly strung together and plastered with mud. The plaster was baked with fire so that the wall became sturdier and more durable.

More than 10,000 productive tools and utensils for daily use have been discovered at Banpo Village. Most are made of stone, including shovels, axes, hoes, knives, adzes, chisels, balls, millstones and fishing-net sinkers; the others are worked-bone tools, such as knives, shovels, awls, needles, arrowheads, fishing hooks and forks. There are earthenware as well, such as spinning wheels and foils. Some of the tools are so finely crafted that it is unbelievable that they were made by people some 6,000 years ago.

Ceramics was an important handicraft for Banpo Man. Utensils for daily use were generally made of red clay mixed with coarse or fine sand, including bowls, basins, jars, kettles, pots, steamers and bottles, but most were coarse sand pots, bowls and jars with a tiny mouth and pointed bottom. Much of the pottery is graced with rope, line, tapering or hooked lines incised either with fingernails or the tip of an awl. The presence of many earthen jars with a pointed bottom is the subject of much study; researchers, having probed deep into their mechanics, maintain that they were used for fetching water.

Painted pottery is a major hallmark of the Banpo branch of Neolithic culture. The patterns, which were often inscribed on both sides of an earthen utensil, cover such motifs as human face, fish, deer and plant as well as geometric patterns like triangles and round dots. This decorative art shows that Banpo Man had already become very aesthetic-conscious.

Another major discovery at Banpo is the hundred or so signs in twenty-odd forms painted on the earthenware. Archaeologists regard them as primitive pictographic characters. Much speculation has been made as to their meanings, an effort which is helpful to the study of the origin of the

10

Chinese written language.

Of the 250 primitive tombs found at Banpo, 174 belonged to the remains of grownups lying straight on their backs. Seventy-three of them belonged to children, whose remains were encoffined in cupped earthen urns, with a tiny hole — believed to be the outlet for the deceased's soul — bored into the bottom of this "combination coffin".

Thanks to a warm and moist climate, Banpo in its primitive days had plenty of water supply and its ground was covered with rich vegetation. The discovery of the fossils of maize from the ruins indicates that farming was already a way of life, supplemented with fishing, hunting and livestock breeding. Experts believe Banpo was a matriarchal society in which production was penurious at best, and people had to stick together to keep natural adversities at bay.

A museum was established on the ruins in 1958. The earliest in situ museum in China, the Xian Banpo Museum provides the visitor who has just marvelled at the consummate cultural achievements of the Zhou, Han and Tang dynasties in and around Xi'an with the opportunity to get lost for a while in a civilization in its crudest and most primitive form.

13

13. The foundation of a round abode. Banpo Man's abodes fall into four types: Round houses built on the ground; cellar-like round houses built half way into the ground; square houses built on the ground; and cellar-like houses built half way into the ground.
14. A painted pottery bowl, looking lovable although it was made for practical use.

14

15

15. Banpo Man fetched water with this pottery amphora which features a pointed bottom and tiny mouth; this kind of pottery amphoras, which have also been discovered at Jiangzhai and other places of the same cultural background, is a representative utensil of the Yangshao Culture.

◀ **16**. A gourd-shaped jar ornamented with pig-face patterns.
17. The five tiny fish painted inside this pottery basin look as if they were swimming in water; fish is a regular motif of the Painted Pottery Culture.

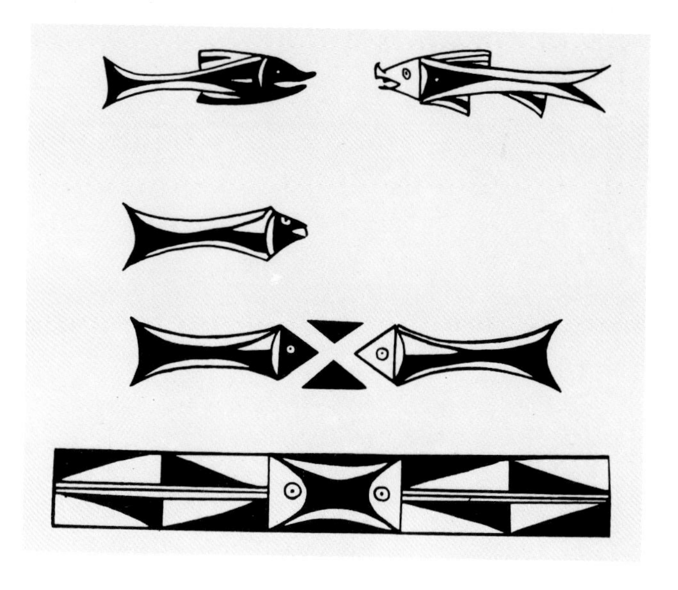

17

18

19

18. A gourd-shaped painted pottery jar, discovered from the Jiangzhai ruins, Lintong County, which belonged to the same period as the ruins at Banpo Village; the jar, graced whith fish designs, looks elegant in a crude way.

19. A gourd-shaped jar ornamented with pig-face patterns.

20. The Banpo Museum of Xi'an is China's first insitu museum which showcases the abodes of Banpo Man.
21. Worked-bone and shell tools and ornaments, which shed some light on Banpo Man's pursuit for beauty.

20

21

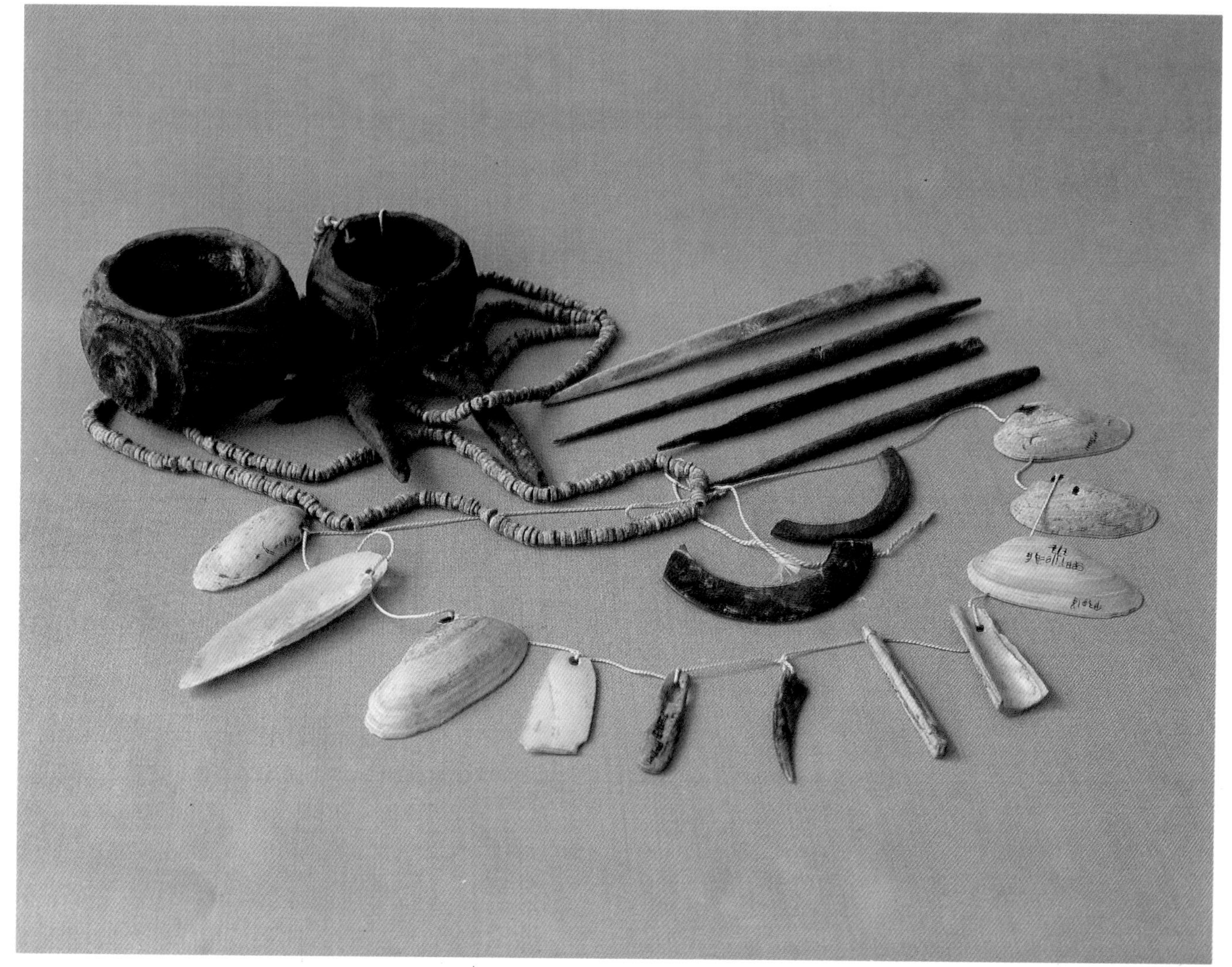

A Millennium's Merry-Go-Round: Capitals of Thirteen Dynasties

In the eventful and venerable Chinese history no city is bathed in such importance and splendour as Xi'an, the venue for imperial capitals of thirteen dynasties beginning from the Western Zhou Dynasty. It is no exaggeration to say that Xi'an epitomizes the first half of Chinese feudal society.

Since the Zhou and Qin dynasties, Xi'an had emerged as the political, economic and cultural centre of China. During the eleventh century BC the Zhou people, who emerged on the political scene as a force to be reckoned with in present-day Qishan and Fufeng counties, conquered the Shang Dynasty and established the first capitals in the Xi'an area — first at Feng and then at Hao. Five centuries late, the Qin people established their capital at Yongcheng, Leyang and Xianyang respectively; when they fought out of Hangu, eliminated six rival states and unified the country for the first time under the Qin empire, Xianyang continued to serve as the capital city. After Liu Bang toppled the Qin Dynasty and made himself Emperor Gaozu of the Han Dynasty, he built his capital at a place opposite Xianyang across the Wei River — he made a wise choice, for the new capital was backed by the fertile eight-hundred-li Qinchuan Plain. When Wang Mang usurped the power of the floundering Western Zhou Dynasty and established his short-lived regime, he inherited the capital and political system of his predecessors. Before long the Yellow Turbans Uprising took place, and Dong Zhuo, who burnt down all the imperial palaces in Luoyang and thus made himself the target of a punitive expedition by eighteen dukes, forced Emperor Xiandi to move his capital to Chang'an, where the Eastern Han Dynasty met its demise six years later. Emperor Mindi of the Western Jin Dynasty took the throne at Chang'an, only to be dethroned by Liu Yao in three years. Then came the Northern Dynasties, and the Early Zhao, Early Qin, Late Qin, Western Wei and Northern Zhou proclaimed Chang'an as the capital in a merry-go-round fashion. After the Anle and Xianghe rebellions during the Han Dynasty, the city of Chang'an was ravaged by the turmoil and chaos of long years of war. In 581 AD, when Yang Jian unified China once again and made himself Emperor Wendi of the Sui Dynasty, the celebrated architect Yu Wenkai masterminded the construction of the Sui capital, Daxing, which surpassed the Han-dynasty Chang'an in both scale and architecture. Chinese history reached its zenith during the Tang Dynasty, and Chang'an, as the capital, was unmatched by any other imperial city in pomp and pageant throughout Chinese history. It was not only the political, economic and cultural centre of the great Tang empire, but also the starting point of the Silk Road Due partly to this road, Chang'an, thronged by merchants from various parts of the world, eventually emerged as the leading international metropolis in the East.

History has lavished its favour upon Xi'an, which has repaid by adding substance and lustre to history. The mere mention of the heyday of the Xi'an known as Chang'an never fails to fill every Chinese with pride. The dazzling array of cultural relics and treasures contained in Xi'an and its vicinity, are inalienable to its venerated position as the country's capital in so many dynastic periods.

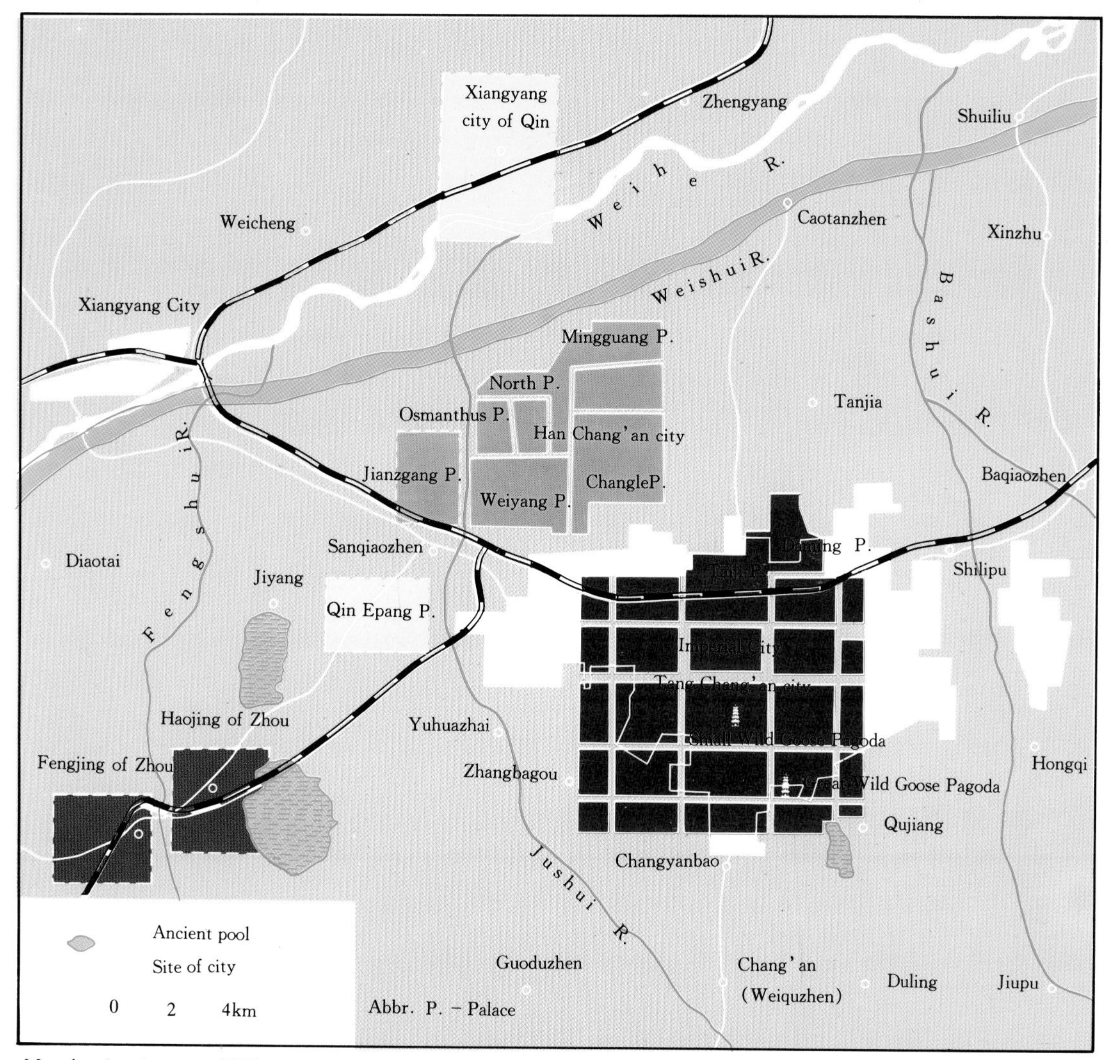

Map showing sites around Xi'an that have served as dynastic capitals in Chinese history.

Imperial capitals in and around Xi'an

Dynasty	Period	Location	Duration (year)
Western Zhou	1121-771 BC	Feng, Hao (present- day Zhangjiapo and Doumenzhen, Chang'an County)	350
Qin	221-207 BC	Xianyang (present-day Yaodianzhen Xianyang)	15
Western Han	206 BC-8 AD	Chang'an (northwest of present-day Xi'an)	214
Xinmang	9-23 AD	Ibid	15
Eastern Han (Emperor Xian)	190-195 AD	Ibid	5
Western Jin (Emperor Mindi)	313-316 AD	Ibid	4
Early Zhao	319-329 AD	Ibid	11
Early Qin	351-384 AD	Ibid	34
Late Qin	386-417 AD	Ibid	32
Western Wei	535-556 AD	Ibid	22
Northern Zhou	557-581 AD	Ibid	25
Sui	581-618 AD	Daxing (present-day Xi'an)	37
Tang	618-907 AD	Chang'an (Ibid)	289

Feng and Hao: Earliest Capitals in Xi'an

22. The Feng River, made enchanting and mysterious by the fact that its shores are strewn with a wealth of cultural treasures dating back to the Western Zhou Dynasty some 3,000 years ago.
23. The ruins of a pit buried with chariots and horses at Zhangjiapo Village on the western shore of the Feng River.
24. Meng's gui, a grain container. One of the heavy-duty Western Zhou vessels exhumed from the ruins of Feng and Hao, it was unearthed from Zhangjiapo on the western bank of the Feng River and is now in the collection of the Shaanxi Provincial History Museum. On its bottom are inscribed with 42 Chinese characters.
25. A jade circumpolar constellation template.

Feng and Hao, which served successively as the capital of the Western Zhou Dynasty during the eleventh century B.C., were situated on the Feng River a dozen kilometres to the southwest of present-day Xi'an.

Historical records show that King Wen of Zhou established his capital at Feng on the western bank of the Feng River and King Wu of Zhou had his capital at Hao on the eastern bank. Since the 1950s the Archaeology Institute of the Chinese Academy of Sciences and archaeological departments in Shaanxi have conducted large-scale surveys and excavations in both ancient capitals. In the intervening years they have verified their general scopes, exhumed dozens of foundations and several hundred tombs, and sorted out a good number of bronzeware from underground cellars, thereby unveiling the mystery that had enshrouded the imperial capitals for more than 3,000 years and the Bronze Culture they represented.

To be exact, Feng was located at today's Keshengzhuang and Mawang Town west of the Feng River. In terms of scale, the foundations uncovered there exceeded the ruins of giant clan temples at nearby Zhouyuan. The largest foundation, covering a space of more than 1,800 square metres in the heart of the capital, is believed to be part of residences of Western Zhou aristocrats.

Hao was located at today's Doumen Town and Huayuan and Pudu villages east of the Feng River. Extensive rammed-earth foundations and such building materials as flat tiles, semitubular tiles and lime plasters have been found since the 1960s. Foundation No. 5, dug up by the Shaanxi Provincial Archaeological Research Institute only recently, is attributed to the largest imperial palace in the Zhou Dynasty. Rectangular flights of rammed-earth steps protrude from all four edges of the foundation, which rises to as high as five metres and whose floor is pockmarked by a high density of round depressions left by rammers.

The ruins of pottery kilns and bone-tool workshops have also been found in both ancient capitals. In 1989, archaeologists found a workshop at Xinwang Village which specialized in the making of worked-bone tools such as hairpins and arrowheads during the late Western Zhou Dynasty; though badly defaced, the ruins belie the large size of the construction.

Clusters of Western-Zhou tombs have been found in Feng and Hao, and several hundred of them have been brought to light in recent decades. For instance, 390 tombs and pits buried with chariots and horses were exhumed during the 1984-85 period at Zhangjiapo in west Feng. These included a large tomb which extends for thirty-five metres north and south in the shape of the Chinese character "zhong", from which large quantities of precious Western-Zhou Bronzeware have been found.

Actually, a wealth of bronzeware is buried underground in the Western-Zhou capitals of Feng and Hao, renowned centres of the Bronze Culture. Apart from sacrificial objects discovered in the above-mentioned tombs, many cellars have been unearthed from beneath the ruins. In 1961, a total of 53 bronze utensils were discovered at Zhangjiapo; and in 1973, another crop of 25 bronzes, including a Wei tripod, was found at the same place. A Duoyou tripod inscribed with a text of more than 200 Chinese characters was found at Xiaquan Village in 1980, and in the following year a 54-kilogramme tripod was exhumed at Xinwang Village. All these are important archaeological findings from the ruins of Feng and Hao.

Due to its remote antiquity and the vicissitudes of the last three millennia, the mystery that envelops the Western-Zhou capitals are yet to be thoroughly unveiled. It can be predicted, however, more stunning archaeological finds will be made at Feng and Hao in the days to come to substantiate the splendid achievements of the Bronze Culture.

22

23

24

25

26. A he, rounded vessel with a closed spout, handle, cover and legs.
27. A hollow piece of jade with rectangular sides.
28. A bronze tripod inscribed with linked fish-hook lines.

26

27

28

Xianyang: Centre of a Unified Em- pire

Located in the centre of the 800-li Qin river valley and northwest of the ancient capital of Chang'an, Xianyang on the shore of the Wei River commands vast tracks of fertile land. Strategically situated, it was the capital of the Qin dynasty, the first centralized feudal monarchy in Chinese history. From 350 BC, when Duke Xiao of Qin moved his capital from Yueyang to Xianyang during the twelfth year of his reign, to the rise and fall of the Qin Dynasty, Xianyang served as the Qin capital for 144 years. In 206 BC, Xiang Yu the Lord of Chu stormed into the city with his army with burning hatred of the Qin Dynasty. In the sack of the city that followed, the mighty Qin capital was reduced to debris.

Since 1959, experts from the Shaanxi Provincial Archaeology Research Institute and other departments have engaged in extensive archaeological surveys and diggings in this place. They have found, among other things, that the Qin-dynasty capital was located east of present-day Xianyang on the northern bank of the Wei River, and that its territory, covering several dozen square kilometres, reached as far as Sanqiao Town south of the Wei River in what is today's Xi'an. The formidable city of Xianyang boasted a mass of imperial palaces and summer resorts, including the legendary Efang Palace, which scrawled on both

29. Tiger Tally, uncovered at Ducheng Village, Chang'an County, which was the territory of the state of Du. The other piece of the tally is missing. The gold-inlaid walking tiger is inscribed with 40 characters in nine lines. Now in the collection of the Shaanxi Provincial History Museum.

30. An ancient ferry crossing at Xianyang.

29

30

31

banks of the Wei River for several hundred li on end; the cityscape was spectacular enough to justify the power and prosperity of the Qin empire.

The Qin imperial palaces now lie in piles of dust at Yaodian Township in present-day Xianyang. Palace Site One is now a high earth mound rimmed with pebble-paved waterways with square-brick edges, and whose south, west and north sides were lined with corridors. Baths were found in the buildings. The main hall was a rough square structure whose vermillion-painted floor covered more than 160 square metres, and a drainage installation is found at the foot of the frontal stairway. The buildings of the 7,000-square-metre Palace Site Three were linked to each other by zigzagging corridors; and vestiges of huge frescos can be discerned on the walls. On the east and west walls, pictures totalling thirty metres in length feature such motifs as buildings, chariots and horses, figures, hunting scenes, birds and animals, plants and fiends painted in every imaginable colour — red, black, purple, brown, blue, green and what not. A large and relatively better preserved fresco about carriages drawn by four horses features a horse-harnessing method similar to the way the painted bronze carriage and horses unearthed from the Qinshihuang Mausoleum are put together. The importance of these frescos speaks for itself as they are the only collection of Qin-dynasty wall paintings left and the earliest palace murals ever known to the world. More fresco fragments have been uncovered from the 4,000 square-metre Palace Site Two along with a drainage pond and a water tank.

The peripheries of former Xianyang palaces, too, abound in cultural relics and historical sites. These include the Qinlan Pond, Efang and Wangyi palaces, workshops and storage cellars. Most of the unearthed artifacts are now preserved in the Xianyang Municipal Museum, the Shaanxi Provincial Archaeological Research Institute and other departments. These include the Xiaguan bell of Anyi, which was a war trophy the Duke of Qin obtained after eliminat-

31. A bronze capacity measurer inscribed with two imperial edicts on Qinshihuang's steps to unify weights and measures after he unified China. Written fastidiously in the small-seal script, the edicts are valuable for both historians and calligraphers.
32. Stone weight of a steelyard.

32

33

34

33. Ruins of the legendary Efang Palace, found north of Sanqiao Town on the western outskirts of Xi'an. Cultural relics are often discovered from the existing large rammed earth foundations.

34. Hollow brick with dragon patterns. As the Chinese saying goes, the Qin Dynasty was known for its bricks and the Han Dynasty for its tiles. Polished to shine and cut in intaglio with dragon and other patterns, this 117-cm hollow brick uncovered from a Qin palace at Xianyang stands as a testimony to the splendour and solemnity of Qin-dynasty Xianyang palaces.

35. Qin-dynasty hollow brick with phoenix patterns.
36. This gold-inlaid bronze tripod stands 13.7 cm tall with a diameter of 11.9 cm. Despite its small size it is a rare piece of bronze metallurgy with an elegant shape and superb craftsmanship. The lid, belly, ears and legs are all inlaid with gold.

ing the state of Wei; Chen Ai's gold talisman, a precious Chu treasure inscribed with the text of the Qin-dynasty ordnance for the unification of the country's weights and measures; frescos discovered from Xianyang palaces; decorative tile-ends in diverse designs, dragon-patterned hollow bricks and other building materials; and large quantities of bronzeware, ironware and ceramics. All these artifacts speak volumes for the wisdom and creativity of the labouring people of the Qin Dynasty and furnish conclusive material evidence for the merits of the state of Qin in unifying the country under a feudal autocracy for the first time in Chinese history.

35

36

37

38

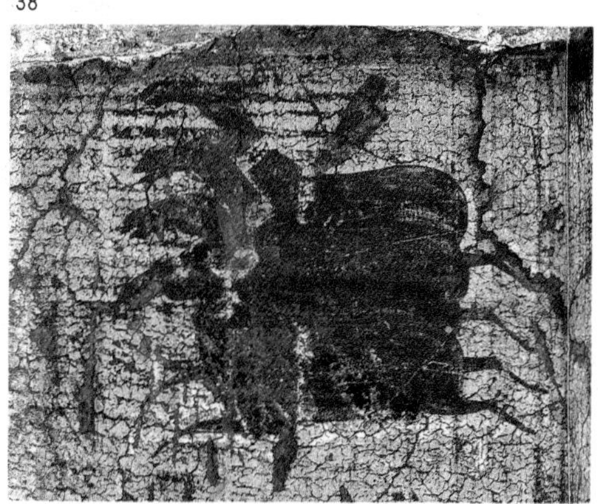

37. Bronze sculpture of a warrior.
38. A Procession of Horse-Drawn Carriages, the earliest palace fresco ever found, was unearthed from Site 3 of the ruins of the Qin-dynasty Xianyang Palace. The fresco, which is partly defaced, portrays three carriages painted in white, each drawn by four galloping horses.

Chang'an: A Full-Fledged Metropolis

The ruins of Chang'an, capital of the Western Han Dynasty (206-23 AD), are found on the northwest outskirts of Xi'an, opposite the Qin-dynasty capital of Xianyang across the Wei River.

In the early years of the Western Han Dynasty, Liu Bang was so impressed by the boundless fertile land of the Guanzhong Plain and its strategic position, that when he took the throne as Emperor Gaozu he had his capital city of Chang'an built on the northern bank of the Wei River. Before long an impressive array of structures emerged, including the Changle and Weiyang palaces, a weaponry and a granary. During the reign of Emperor Wudi of the Han Dynasty, the Guigong and Mingguang palaces were added, the famous Kunming Lake was dug and the Zhanggong Palace constructed by it. After Wang Mang usurped the power in the late Western Han Dynasty, he added the Mingtang Palace and a number of ritual installations.

During the Han Dynasty Chang'an was the political, economic and cultural centre of China as well as an international city which stood comparison with such booming cities as Rome. During the reign of Emperor Wu, Chang'an found itself at the starting point of the celebrated Silk Road opened up by Zhang Qian, and, riding the high tide of thriving trade and economic ties between Europe and Asia, the city achieved unprecedented prosperity.

Since 1956 the Archaeology Institute of the Chinese Academy of Sciences has organized systematic surveys of the Han-dynasty Chang'an. Having unearthed the city walls and gates, the Changle, Weiyang and Shaofu palaces and the arsenal, researchers and scholars succeeded in defining the general plan of the ancient capital.

The Han-dynasty Chang'an features a near square layout, covering thirty-six square kilometres with a circumference of 25.7 kilometres. The moated city wall was a rammed-earth structure twelve metres in height, but the elements have reduced the existing parts to ridges 0.8-2 metres high (8.3 metres at the highest) and 12-16 metres wide at the base. Of the wall's twelve gates, the positions of the Jinba, Xi'an, Fu'ang, Xuanping, Luocheng, Chucheng, Zhicheng and Zhangcheng gates are relatively clear, and the Bacheng Gate is the best preserved; but because some

40

wall sections are missing, the positions of the Anmen, Qingming, Hengmen and Yongmen gates can only be roughly estimated. A network of eight streets with a general width of 45 metres ran across the city in addition to a main road reserved for the emperor's exclusive use. Anmen Street, the central street, ran north and south for 5,500 metres as the longest in town. Palaces, yamens and residential mansions covered the bulk of the city space. The largest palace, Changle, spread on an area of about six square kilometres. The arsenal was found between the Changle and the Weiyang places. The Guigong and Northern palaces stood north of the Weiyang Palace, while the Mingguang Palace was found north of the Changle Palace in the city's northeast part.

The ruins of the Weiyang Palace, the Western Han administrative centre, were discovered at Weiyanggong Township, Xi'an. Large amounts of artifacts and historical sites have been found there, thanks to repeated efforts of the Archaeology Institute of the Chinese Academy of Sciences. In the centre of a palace complex the Frontal Hall lies in debris on a rammed-earth foundation whose northern part is higher than its southern part and which measures 405 metres long from north to south and 185 metres wide from east to west; with its three major halls poised on a high

39

39. Ruins of the frontal hall which was the centrepiece of the Weiyang Palace on the northwestern outskirts of Xi'an. A large rammed-earth platform is left there, surrounded by a number of Western Han structures, now in ruins.
40. The Jianzhang Palace.
41. Painted pottery wild goose.
42. A of gold-plated bronze paper weights in the shape of a peacock were excavated in the western suburb of Xi'an in 1989. The squatting peacock looks vivid with its head turned to peck at its wings.

41

foundation this palace was laid out tastefully according to the contours of the Longshou Hill. The area surrounding the Weiyang Palace's foundation is strewn with a host of minor foundations, all in ruins. These include the Jiaofang Hall in the Rear Palace (residence for the empress), the Shiju and Tianlu pavilions, office of the Ministry of Labour, and the Chamber of Palace Revenues. From the ruins of the Ministry of Labour tens of thousands of worked-bone slips six-seven by two-three cm were found in-

42

43. Decorative tile-ends with dragon patterns. In ancient times, the Green Dragon, White Tiger, Scarlet Bird and Black Tortoise were regarded as the protective gods in the four directions. Crafted in good taste, these tile-ends reflect the artistic trends of the people of the Han Dynasty.
44. A tile-end with tiger patterns.
45. A tile-end with Scarlet Bird patterns.
46. A tile-end with Black Tortoise designs.

the southern outskirts of the Han-dynasty Chang'an. These include the Hall of Enlightened Rule built during the Yuanshi Reign near the ruler's palace as a symbol of dynastic legitimacy and sovereignty, "Wang Mang's Nine Temples" erected during the Xinmang Reign, as well as circular altars and the Altar of the Land and Grain. Their ruins are well preserved save for those which have given way to modern constructions.

The ruins of an earthenware workshop, covering 14, 000 square metres, have been found in the northwestern corner of the Han-dynasty Chang'an. From the site archaeologists unearthed what is remained of a kiln alongside pottery figurines in sitting and kneeling positions, some of scribed in different numbers of characters with years,

43 44 45 46

names of ministry officials and state labourers and lists of materials and objects. This discovery with its sheer number and high academic value sufficed to make archaeology history.

The arsenal consisted of seven warehouses, in which the imperial army kept its weapons. The warehouses were of different sizes but had the same rectangular design, with a door opened into each of the four walls. From the arsenal weapons and daily utensils were discovered along with foundation stones, bricks and tiles, and charcoal ashes. The weapons are made of iron or bronze, including swords, spears, axes, knives, and dagger axes.

Lying in ruins too are a number of ritual buildings on

which are portrayed in nudity, as well as pottery animals. These figurines are similar to those unearthed from the Yangling Mausoleum of Han Emperor Jingdi in terms of imagery and conception. It is speculated that this workshop specialized in making figurines as sacrificial burial objects for the emperor's mausoleum.

Since 1956, archaeological excavation and studies of the Han-dynasty Chang'an have continued unabated. To the above-mentioned sites and relics have been added many other discoveries. They combine to form a precious cultural legacy which reflects the prosperity and vitality of an empire of bygone days and showcases the labouring people's wisdom and indelible contributions to world civilization.

Peak of Glory: Tang-dynasty Chang'an

Built on the basis of the Sui-dynasty capital of Daxing, the Tang-dynasty capital of Chang'an covered eighty-three square kilometres, eight times as big as the city proper of present-day Xi'an which looks more or less the same as it did during the Ming Dynasty. As a masterpiece of Sui-and-Tang architecture and city planning, the Tang-dynasty capital is aptly described in this line: "Houses in their hundreds and thousands are arrayed in chessboard fashion, criss-crossed by twelve streets in a way reminiscent of a vegetable plot." All the palaces and houses and roads were arranged according to a well-conceived plan to fit the position of the Tang-dynasty Chang'an as the nation's political, economic and cultural centre and as one of the world's most populous and thriving cities.

A comprehensive survey of the ancient capital came under way in 1957. Experts from the Archaeology Institute of the Chinese Academy of Sciences conducted systematic diggings of the sites of some major imperial palaces, houses and temples, thereby gaining detailed knowledge of the layout and scope of the entire city.

The Tang Chang'an consisted of the outer city, the inner city, imperial city, neighbourhoods and two markets. The inner city and the imperial city to its south were found in the middle of the northern part of the outer city. The east and west markets were situated in the southeast and south of the imperial city respectively. The streets were aligned in an orderly fashion, and the entire layout was a well-knit, self-containing enclosure balanced symmetrically on a meridian line. The outer city, with a circumference of 36.7 kilometres, was 9,721 metres long from east to west and 8,651.7 metres wide from north to south. Unfortunately, very little has been left of the moated city wall which once stood twelve metres high. Vestiges of brick walls are found where the city gates used to be.

The inner city situated in the central-north of the outer city measures 1,492.1 metres long from north to south and 2,820.3 metres wide from east to west, with a perimeter of more than 8.6 kilometres. In its centre stood the Palace of the Supreme Being, where the emperor handled state affairs. To the south of the inner city was the imperial city, 1,843.6 metres long from north to south and as wide as the inner city, with a circumference of 9.2 kilometres. The Zhuque (Scarlet Bird) Gate was opened into the middle of the southern edge of the imperial city, the starting point of Zhuque boulevard which ran southward to form the meridian line of the entire city of Chang'an. The outer city boasted eleven streets that ran north and south and fourteen boulevards which ran east and west. All the roads were wide, with the central Zhuque Boulevard being the most magnificent with a width of 150 to 155 metres. The city was divided up into 110 neighbourhoods according to a regular layout, and the two commercial centres, the east and west markets, were properly positioned in the city, which also had four water-supplying canals running through it. Added to the cluster of imperial gardens and parks was the Qujiang Lake, a well-known scenic spot which rent peace and repose to the boisterous life of the Tang capital.

Basing themselves on systematic surveys, archaeologists and scholars organized excavation work on a number of major sites, including the Palace of Great Brightness, the Xingqing Palace, and the Qinglong and Ximing temples.

As part of the forbidden city, the Palace of Great Brightness is situated on Longshou Terrace in the northeastern part of the imperial capital. When it was first completed in 634 AD, or the eighth year of the Zhenguan Reign, it was known as Yong'an Palace. In 662 AD, the second year of the Longshuo Reign, Emperor Gaozong had it expanded; the following year he gave it the present name and began presiding over court sessions there. Before it was burned down during the war in 896 AD, or the third year of the Qianning Reign, the Palace of Great Brightness used to be the grandest of all Ming-dynasty palaces. Covering an area of 3.2 square kilometres with a circumference of 7.6 kilometres, the inner city alone had eleven gates and its east, west and north sides were fortified with double walls, while the south side was screened with three tall walls and made accessible with Danfengmen Boulevard which ran as wide as 176 metres. The Hanyuan Hall was the centrepiece of the entire palace. Ruins of the Institute of Literateurs and the hall of Pure Trinity have also been discovered in the palace.

The Hanyuan Hall was where the emperor presided over major celebrations and ceremonies, but today only a platform was left of it, protruding from the ground for fifteen metres. A survey shows that the foundation is 75.9 metres long from east to west and 41.3 metres wide from north to south, and the hall, eleven bays wide and four bays deep, was guarded by the Tower of Flying Phoenix and the Phoenix Perching tower which towered fifteen metres over the main hall to its southeast and southwest. Three ramps conducted to the south side of the hall, and large amounts of broken bricks, tiles, stone pillars, horn-less stone dragon heads, iron armours and spearheads have been dug up from the foundation. Situated to the west of the Palace of Great Brightness and measuring 130 metres long north and south and 80 metres wide from east to west, the Institute of Literateurs situated to the west of the Palace of Great Brightness was divided up into frontal, central and rear chambers, covering a total space of 12,300 square metres. Bricks, tiles and horn-less stone dragon heads and other building materials have been unearthed there. The roof of the hall was covered with black-glazed tiles, and the passageways and steps were covered with square bricks carved with lotus flower patterns, and the waterways were paved with black square bricks — all being rare examples in Chinese architecture.

The Hall of Pure Trinity situated in the northwest corner of the Palace of Great Brightness has only a fifteen-metre-high foundation left today, which features a 4,000-square-metre convex floor 78.6 metres long from north to south and 53.1-47.6 metres wide from east to west. This was where Taoist ceremonies were held. Archaeologists have also discovered the sites of some other halls in the palace complex such as the Hall for Buddhist Affairs, the Hall of Purple Throne and the hall of Pure Benevolence.

The Xingqing Palace was yet another palatial complex

47. The ruins of Linde Hall, Daming Palace.

A Map of Tang-Dynasty Chang'an

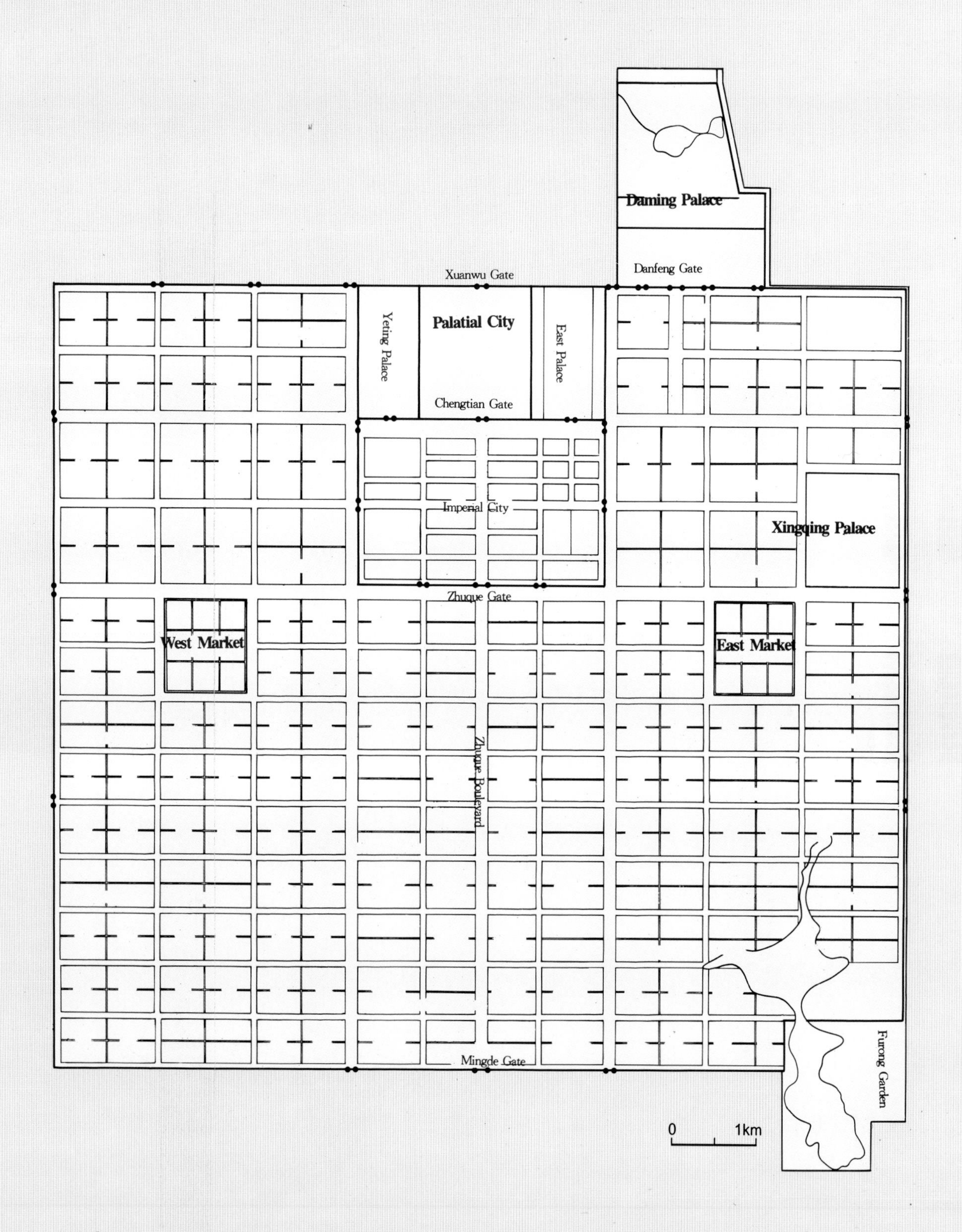

48

48. A tri-coloured horseback-riding figurine. Exhumed from the western suburb of Xi'an in 1975, the figurine is portrayed in the image of an affable northern tribesman sitting astride the back of a galloping horse. The man and the horse set each other off in a pleasing contrast.

49

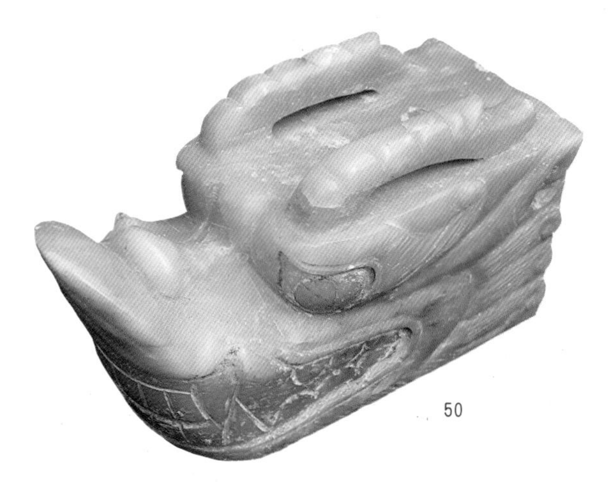

50

49. Imperial Lady Yang's bath, in the shape of a crabapple tree leaf.
50. White jade carving of the head of a dragon.
51. The pompous lifestyle behind the walls of the Tang imperial palaces is revealed in this gold-plated door-knocker, unearthed from the ruins of the Tang-dynasty Daming Palace.

51

in Chang'an. Situated at what is today's Xingqinggong Park, the palace was separated by a double wall from the Palace of Great Brightness. In 728 AD, or the sixteenth year of the Kaiyuan Reign, Emperor Xuanzong moved to this palace to handle court affairs, thereby turning it into the country's political centre and a permanent residence for the emperor and his beloved concubines. The Xingqing Palace was an rectangular structure divided into northern and southern palaces. The southern palace was an providently landscaped garden with the Dragon Pond in the centre; and the northern palace was where the various halls were located. The entire palace complex was surrounded by a wall more than 1,000 metres long on each of the four sides; and its space of 1.35 square kilometres was taken up by the the Tower of the Essentials for Diligent Government, the Xingqing Hall, the Datong Hall, the Chenxiang Pavilion and other buildings. The Tower of the Essentials for Diligent government, the centrepiece of the entire complex, was so named as to reflect Emperor Xuanzong's desire to "be diligent with political affairs and sympathetic with the populace" . The Chenxiang Pavilion was where Emperor Xuanzong feasted and frolicked with his charming Imperial Lady Yang.

Monasteries and Taoist temples were another salient feature of the Tang-dynasty Chang'an. Excavations of such sites as the Ximing (West Brightness) and Qinglong (Green

52

53. The Huaqing Palace, a major summer resort for Tang-dynasty emperors. For many years this was where Li Longui or Emperor Xuanzong and his favorite concubine Imperial Lady Yang enjoyed each other's company. Ruins of the baths used by the emperor and the lady and the crown prince have been found there, and a museum has been established on the ruins of the Huaqing Palace.
54. Nanxun chamber, Xingqing Palace.
55. The pottery sculpture of a servant maid, molded in the typical image of Tang-dynasty females. Looking plump, serene and full of youthful energy, this image is similar to Tang-dynasty beauties portrayed in tomb frescos, stone-carved portraiture and grotto murals, and it reflects the Tang-dynasty obsession with fatness.

53

55 ▶

Dragon) temples have yielded a rich harvest of religious objects and building materials.

The Tang-dynasty Chang'an, laid out symmetrically along a meridian line according to a regular plan on the basis of the Sui capital of Daxing, was a pioneering effort in ancient Chinese city planning and construction. It had a population of more than one million, over and above foreigners who arrived by the thousand along the Silk Road. The prosperous, powerful and yet fastidiously administered Chang'an of the Tang Dynasty was, indeed, a vivid embodiment of a period of unrivaled splendour and prosperity in Chinese history.

54

The Twilight:
In Post-Sui and Tang Years

After the demise of the Sui and Tang dynasties, the political and cultural centre of the country was moved southward. Chang'an lost its position as the national capital, but remained as the provincial capital of and largest city in Shaanxi, a province which was vital to the central government's control of the entire northwest.

During the Song and Jin dynasties, Chang'an was known as Commandery of the North Capital or Metropolitan Prefecture. With a position a cut above other prefectures, the city's jurisdiction extended for a time to part of present-day Henan and Shanxi provinces. During the Yuan Dynasty, Shaanxi Province with Chang'an as the centre encompassed Shaanxi, east Gansu and part of Ningxia and Inner Mongolia; by the time of Prince Anxi, Chang'an had became the headquarters of an all-mighty 150,000-strong army whose sphere of influence encompassed Hexi, Tubo and Sichuan. Zhu Yuanzhang, the founding emperor of the Ming Dynasty, dispatched his son on an inspection tour of

Shaanxi in the belief that "of all the mountains and plains, the Qin Plain is of most strategic importance" . In 1369, or the second year of the Hongwu Reign of the Ming Dynasty, Chang'an was renamed Xi'an. The original name, Chang'an, was restored briefly in 1643, or the sixteenth year of the Chongzhen Reign, when Li Zicheng's peasant rebels captured the city. During the Ming Dynasty, Xi'an was the seat of a provincial administrative commission in charge of Shaanxi, most of Gansu and part of Qinghai, Ningxia and Inner Mongolia. During the Qing Dynasty, the city became the seat of the Sichuan-Shaanxi Viceroy in charge of garrison troops in Shaanxi, Sichuan, Gansu and Shanxi. The importance of Xi'an in these periods was self-evident.

Towards the end of the Tang Dynasty, as a result of the Coup of Zhu Wen, Emperor Zhaozong was forced to move east to Luoyang, and the ancient city of Chang'an suffered heavy destruction. Despite repeated repairs and refurbishments during the Song, Yuan, Ming and Qing dynasties, the city failed to recover the scale and prosperity it once knew during the Tang years. What put Chang'an back on the map of Chinese culture during the Song Dynasty was the formation of the Xi'an Stele Forest, the country's largest library-on-stones and treasurehouse of Chinese calligraphy. The mammoth Stele Forest came into shape when Lu Dazhong and others moved more than a hundred stone tablets inscribed with the full text of the Kaicheng Cannon on Stones and a number of other famous Tang-dynasty stone inscriptions to a place east of the Chang'an Academy. In 1370, or the third year of the Hongwu Reign, Zhu Yuanzhang made his second son Zhu Shuang Prince of Qin and put him in command of military and political affairs in northwest China. During the Hongwu Reign, an assortment of imposing structures were built, such as the Ming-dynasty city wall and the drum and bell towers, which have remained to this day. Construction of the Xi'an city wall commenced in 1374, or the seventh year of the Hongwu Reign, and was completed four years later. The east and west walls extend for 2, 600 metres while the north and south walls exceeded 3,200 metres, and the entire city wall measures 13. 75 kilometres in circumference, 12 metres in height, and 12-14 metres wide in its upper part. Four doors are let into the moated city wall, fortified with 98 beacons and 5,984 battlements. The impregnability of such a sturdy defence work was vindicated during the Republican years (1911-1949). When Liu Zhenhua, a Henan warlord, besieged Xi'an for months but failed to conquer it despite his repeated offensives. The Ming-dynasty Xi'an city is by far the only large fortification preserved in its entirety; it is also a miracle in Chinese architecture history. Over the years the Xi'an municipal government has ladled out a hefty amount of money to restore Xi'an to its ancient looks. The city wall, gates and moat are placed under careful protection, and the fabled ancient capital is more or less restored to its former splendor.

The Bell Tower built in 1384 or the seventeenth year of the Hongwu Reign stands towering over the intersection of two major streets in the centre of Xi'an. It is a two-storeyed square wooden structure elevated for thirty-six metres on a thirty-metre square pedestal, looking glorious and serenely elegant with vermillion eaves and green-glazed tiles and a glistening gilded rooftop. A Ming-dynasty cast-iron bell is hung on the second floor to announce time for the entire city.

57

56. City wall of Xi'an during the Ming Dynasty.
57. West city gate of the Ming-dynasty Xi'an.

The Drum Tower built in 1380 or the thirteenth year of the Hongwu Reign stands on the northern side of Xida Street and faces the Bell Tower in the distance. Poised on a gigantic brick foundation with arches opened into its south and north sides, the tower stands thirty-four metres tall, fifty-two metres long from east to west and thirty-seven metres wide from north to south. A large drum was placed on the second floor during the Ming and Qing dynasties to mark time at night. Like the Bell Tower, the Drum Tower also looks solemn and elegant with its rich piles of elaborate ornamentations. The skyline of Xi'an would never looked the same without these two towering structures which echo each other in perfect harmony.

Nothing significant happened in Xi'an from the Qing Dynasty to the early Republican years. It was the Xi'an Incident of the 1930s that refreshed the Chinese memory of this ancient city. On December 12, 1936, Generals Zhang Xueliang and Yang Hucheng shocked the world and wrote a heroic chapter in modern Chinese history6 by launching the Xi'an Incident, which catalyzed the formation of a national united front to counterattack invading Japanese troops. The former sites and structures associated with this incident both in Xi'an and at the nearby Lishan Mountain in Lintong are well preserved for public viewing.

58. The Ming-dynasty Bell Tower.
59. The Ming-dynasty Drum Tower. ▶

58

Mammoth Necropolises: Tombs of Ancient Monarchs

If history had chosen Xi'an as the imperial capital and turned it into the centre stage for a millennium of Chinese political, economic and cultural development, then it was the emperors themselves who dug deep into the yellow earth of the vast Guanzhong Plain in the hope of perpetuating their good old days in the netherworld. The result has been a cultural phenomenon unseen elsewhere in this world — the land of Xi'an is strewn with of all manners of imperial tombs.

The mausoleum of Yellow Emperor, indisputably the father of the Chinese nation, is the earliest of all the imperial tombs so far discovered in Shaanxi. Every year since time immemorial his descendents would return from wherever they live and gather at the top of the Qiaoshan Mountain in Huangling County north of Xi'an to offer libations and sacrifices to him. Apart from Yellow Emperor, more than seventy Chinese emperors from the Western Zhou to the Tang Dynasty are buried in the vicinity of Xi'an. Due to the fact that by tradition no marks were left on burial grounds in the pre-Qin period, the tombs of some of the monarchs are yet to be found out. But most of the imperial tombs built in later years have been identified on the outskirts of the ancient city of Xi'an. Many of them are accompanied by quite a few attendant tombs buried with members of the royal family and trusted generals and officials. Thus a single imperial mausoleum often sprawls over several dozen square kilometres. This has prompted the joke that if all these mausoleums were exhumed, little room would be left for the living.

Because the emperor believed in the immortality of soul and regarded death as another form of life, he tended to go to all lengths to build himself an ideal tomb, and for this purpose he taxed all his ingenuity as if he were dealing with the peace and security of his rule. When his desire for longevity in this world was about to evaporate into thin air, he would choose to seek immortality in the hope of preserving his supreme authority and life of debauchery and dissipation in the other world. Thus elaborate and grandiose funerals became all the rage and the construction of imperial tombs grew in scale and cost. Each imperial tomb was a veritable underground palace, where the extravagance of the living world was reproduced as closely to reality as possible. It is for this very reason that an imperial tomb which lies safely under green mountains and yellow earth always yields more conclusive historical evidence than those whose pomp of architecture and sculpture on the ground courted cruel destruction from man and nature.

Among all the imperial tombs in Xi'an, the mausoleums for Qinshihuang and Han and Tang emperors are more impressive in size, as befitting the fact that under their rules Chinese feudalism emerged, developed and reached its zenith. A thriving economy and the availability of rich material resources inevitably induced the emperor to act out his obsession with luxurious funerals and a comfortable otherworldly existence. To bring every secret about them to light depends on further progress in scholarly studies and archaeological excavations. However, even our partial knowledge is enough to impress our readers with the extent of politics, economics and culture of ancient Chinese society and acquaint them with something about the special position the ancient city of Xi'an holds in traditional Chinese culture.

60. Qinshihuang's Mausoleum.
61. Bronze Carriage No. 1 at Qinshihuang's Mausoleum.
62. Bronze Carriage No. 2 at Qinshihuang's Mausoleum.

60

Largest Mausoleum, Terracotta War- riors

Just as Qinshihuang is regarded as an emperor in his own right, his mausoleum is one of a kind among all the imperial tombs.

The mausoleum is situated in Lintong County thirty-five kilometres east of Xi'an, looking like an awesome peak with the Lishan Mountain rising in the background to the south and the Wei River flowing by in the north. Under morning glow the mausoleum and the mountain are perfectly blended into an integral whole, while the last rays of the setting sun render the premises considerable dignity. Today, the Qinshihuang Mausoleum is both a subject of key government protection and an item on the UNESCU's list of world-class cultural heritages.

Qinshihuang was the first emperor of feudal China. According to history books, he started building the tomb for himself on the Lishan Mountain immediately after he became a king at the tender age of thirteen, But only after he had unified the country in 221 BC could its construction come into full swing. For a time he conscripted as many as 700,000 craftsmen and convicts for the project, going much farther than Khufu of Egypt who had a 146.5-metre-high Pyramid constructed for himself. Yet it still took thirty-eight years to bring his tomb to completion. In Records of the Historian: Biography of Qinshihuang the Han historian Sima Qian wrote that the burial chamber was dug beyond three layers of subterranean water and bronze was cast into it to protect the coffins from water. The tomb contained palaces and pavilions and was filled with rare gems and other treasures. Crossbows were installed which could shoot automatically at tomb robbers. Mercury was pumped in to create images of flowing rivers and surging oceans. The ceiling was ornamented to imitate the sun, the moon and the stars in the sky; and the floor was arranged to simulate the nine divisions of the country and the five holy mountains. All the childless palace maids were killed and buried with the remains of the emperor, and all the artisans who had worked inside the tomb were slaughtered so that none of its secrets was divulged.

After a series of geological explorations and surveys beginning from the 1960s, archaeologists concluded that the tumulus of the mausoleum had an original height of 115 metres, and that the foundation of the mausoleum is a rammed-earth structure in the shape of an inverted dou which measures, at the base, 345 metres wide from east to west and 350 metres long from north to south. Today, having weathered the ravage of the elements and human factors over the last two millennia, the tumulus has shrunk to a height of sixteen metres. Most of the surface structures, such as the inner and outer walls, archways, the memorial hall and its flanks, have crumbled of age and become piles of dust, but the rich hoard of treasures hidden underground remains intact to this day. The centre of the underground palace where the deceased emperor's sepulchre is placed lies about thirty metres below the ground. Because the tomb has never been exhumed, so far there is no knowing of the actual structures of the underground palace. However, more than four hundred attendant burial pits and tombs in different shapes, structures and implications have been verified

61

62

63. Large decorative tile-end graced in high relief with the designs of a kui-dragon and a phoenix in full and smooth lines. Measuring 43 cm tall and with a diameter of 61 cm, it was found in Qinshihuang's Mausoleum and is extolled as "King of Tile-ends" for its sheer size.
64 Pit One of Terracotta Warriors.
65. Bronze shield, 36.2 by 24 cm, a component part of Bronze Carriage No. 1 from Qinshihuang's Mausoleum. The centre of its front features vertical ridges whilethe centre of its back is fixed with a bridge-shaped handle and its both sides are graced with splendid tracery. It furnishes important information for the study of defence weapons in use in ancient China.

63

64

on an area of 56.25 square kilometres. Entombed in these pits and graves are bronze carriages and horses fashioned exactly in the same style as the emperor had seen in his life, precious birds and exotic animals which symbolize His Highness's hunting ground, horse barns, and terracotta warriors and horses arrayed in the fashion of the million-strong army of the Qin empire. So far more than 5,000 important historical relics have been dug up from the site, quite a few of them beng invaluable rarities, such as terracotta renditions of civilian officials and kneeling warriors, gold-inlaid musical bells and decorative tile-ends with kui-dragon designs. Particularly noteworthy is the discovery in December 1980 of two painted bronze horse-drawn carriages, which are by far the biggest and most elegantly ornamented ancient bronze carriages whose structures and harnessing method are fashioned exactly in the same way as in real life. Both are assembled with 3,000-odd component parts, over 1,000 of them being gold and silver. Praised as "King of Bronzes" , they are marked for their graphic images, exquisite craftsmanship, rich gold and silver inlays and elaborate ornamentations of dragon and phoenix patterns.

All the ring-side reports about the attendant burial pits and all the written records on the inside of the underground palace indicate that the Qinshihuang Mausoleum is a copy of the empire the emperor personally shaped and ruled in his lifetime, and he died with the wishful thought that in the darkness of this underground world, he could continue to rule supreme, go hunting or inspecting his subjects, wear his Dawu sword, ride his famed Qianli steeds, and that he

65

66. One of the 116 pairs of saddle horse and terracotta cavalrymen unearthed from Pit Two; the ćavalryman, with reign in hand, is 180 cm tall, and the horse behind him is 172 cm tall and 203 cm long.
67. One of 170 terracotta archers dressed in light war robe, extending one hand forward in a fist and placing another on his chest as if in the process of drawing his bow.
68. Pit Two of Terracotta Warriors.

66

67

could still sit high on his throne and read and endorse reports and proposals, devise strategies for ruling the nation, visit his favorite concubines in the rear palaces, listen to music, or receive the tribute from his officials and objects — all in all, in the other world his imperial rule could continue unabated.

The entombed terracotta warriors discovered 1.5 kilometres east of the Qinshihuang Mausoleum is by far the most important archaeological discovery in this colossal necropolis. Having given our brief introduction to the mausoleum itself, now lets take a look at the mighty imperial army buried some 2,200 years ago.

The pits are found accidentally in 1974 by peasants in the process of drilling a well. There are three of them, arranged in the fashion of the Chinese character "ping" . Pit One, 230 by 62 metres, is the largest, its 14,260-square-metre floor occupied by a mighty formation of 6,000-odd terracotta figurines and horses and 40-odd chariots in four sections: the vanguard, the main force, flanks and the rear guard. Twenty metres to the east of Pit One and about five metres underground lies Pit Two in the shape of a carpenter's square 124 by 98 metres, with a total floorspace of about 6,000 square metres. Buried in this pit are 89 wooden chariots and pottery renditions of 356 draught horses, 116 cavalry horses, and 900 or so warriors holding various weapons in their hands; the formation of infantry, cavalry and chariots is divided into four tiny sections. The vanguard is composed of 172 archers standing in their war robes and 160 heavily armoured archers kneeling with crossbow in hand. The second section, located on the right side of the formation, is composed of 64 horse-drawn chariots each mounted with three soldiers. The third, situated in the cen-

68

69

tre of the entire formation, is a rectangular section in which 19 chariots are placed among a tiny number of infantry and cavalry soldiers. The fourth section on the left of the formation is also rectangular with 108 mounted warriors. Pit Two featuring a formation more complicated and varied than Pit One, is the best of the three in terms of research and aesthetic value. Pit Three, situated 25 metres north of Pit One and 120 metres east of Pit Two, is the smallest, and its 500-square-metre floorspace in the shape of the Chinese character "wa" is divided into south, north and central sections linked with a long corridor. The central section contains a chariot, and the other two sections are manned with varying numbers of terracotta warriors who sit facing each other in two lines, with such ritual weapons as javelins and halberts in their hands. Deer horns and animal bones have also been found. Pit Three appears to be the commanding post for the military formations in the other two pits.

This unprecedented assemblage, in which the terracotta warriors in three services seem ready to spring into action any time, is a vivid microcosm of Qinshihuang's powerful army of "a million armoured soldiers, a thousand war chariots and ten thousand mounted cavalrymen" , with the crack force riding an adreline high with chariots rumbling and horses neighing, and the heavily guarded commanding post busy planning strategies that would insure victory a thousand miles away. Thus the mighty army of an empire 2,200 years is brought into vivid life in the shape of terracotta figurines. For lifelike effects, the builders armed all the warriors with real bronze weapons. Although excavations have so far been limited to part of the huge collection, a total of 30,000 Qin-dynasty weapons have already been brought to light in a dozen or so varieties such as swords, spears, dagger axes, javelins and halberts. Moreover, through the cunning work of the craftsmen, the images of the warriors look so real they seem ready to step out at one's beckoning. Small wonder the entombed warriors are nicknamed "Eighth Wonder in the World" . They are gems contributed by ancient Chinese labouring people to world civilization. Each and every warrior has an undying artistic appear as a paradigm of chivalrous gallantry and heroism.

69 Pit One of Terracotta Warriors.
70. One of the 160 armoured terracotta archers in a kneeling position, bow in hand, found only in Pit Two.

71. A terracotta warrior's head.
The head of a terracotta warrior is often the most vividly portrayed in Qing-dynasty pottery sculpture. Each warrior wears a different facial expression, happy, angry, or sad, some smiling faintly to show an outgoing personality, and some with eyebrows tightly knit as if lost in a reverie. Some look handsome in an innocent way, some have deep-set eyes and flowing beards in the manner of a bookish general. The variegated facial expressions and physiognomy reflect different ages, ethnic backgrounds and personality of soldiers of the Qin army.

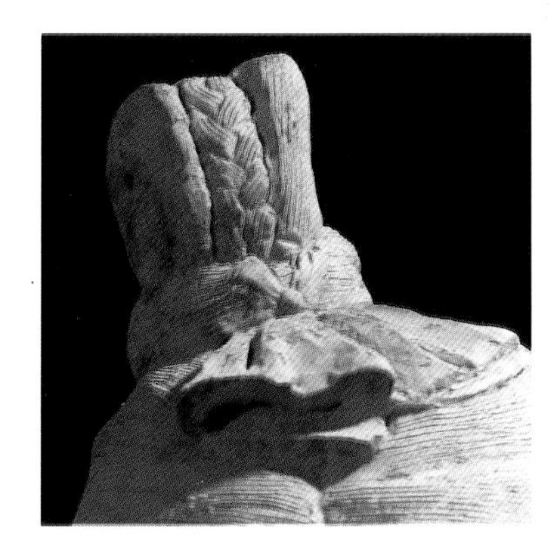

72

Western-Han Imperial Tombs

Of the eleven Western Han emperors from Liu Bang (Emperor Gaozu) to Liu Kan (Emperor Pingdi), nine are buried at Yuanshang, a place north of Xi'an known for its high latitude and thick soil layers. The exceptions were Liu Heng (Emperor Wendi), who was buried at Baling Tableland east of Xi'an, and Liu Xun (Emperor Xuandi), whose remains are lying under Duling Tableland southeast of Xi'an. Looking north from a train on the Lianyungang-Lanzhou Railway, the traveller invariably sees a string of pyramids which are actually the tombs of emperors and empresses. Despite the passage of time, they remain intact on the northern bank of the Wei River, forming a skyline paradoxically desolate and majestic, awful and solemn.

All the tombs were built in an elaborate fashion to serve as emblems of the deceased emperors' luxurious life and aspirations. History books show that an emperor inevitably began building a tomb for himself a year after he took the throne and that one third of the tax-payers' money was used for this purpose. To justify the immortality of their names and the supremacy of their power, they had their sepulchres placed in palaces built deep into the ground, which was marked by a massive tumulus in the shape of an inverted dou. The coffins of emperor and the empress shared the same tumulus but were buried in separate chambers. Most imperial mausoleums are accompanied by varying numbers of attendant tombs buried with the remains of imperial relatives and major officials and generals. The Changling Mausoleum of Liu Bang or Emperor Gaozu is studded with seventy-odd such attendant tombs, so that in death the emperor still had the attention and service of his confidantes such as Xiao He, Cao Can, Zhou Bo, Wang

72. Hollow brick carved with the image of the Scarlet Bird, 110 cm long — This piece of building material of the Han Dynasty was found in the Maoling Mausoleum in Xingping County. On its surface are inscribed with a back-to-back couple of Scarlet Birds on the verge of flying away, their combs erect and their wings open, with one foot placed in front of the other.
73. The Yangling Mausoleum for Emperor Jingdi of the Han Dynasty.
74. The Maoling Mausoleum for Emperor Wudi of Han.
75. Han-dynasty terracotta warriors discovered at Yangjiawan Village. About 3,000 such warriors have been unearthed from an attendant burial pit of the Changling Mausoleum of Liu Bang, or Emperor Gaozu of the Han Dynasty. Among them the number of infantrymen is the largest, and the number of cavalrymen is the second largest. Each warrior wears a black armour atop clothes in red, white or yellow. This mighty army is marked for graphic imagery and arranged in neat formations, which shed light on the weapons and military formations of the Han Dynasty in its early years.

73

74

75

76. Hollow brick inscribed with the design of the Black Tortoise, approximately 117 cm long — Unearthed from the Maoling Mausoleum in Xingping County, the brick is carved with the images of a tortoise and a snake facing each other. The tortoise is depicted in an energetic image, with head protruding and eyes wide open and four legs in the process of making a stride. The composition is most spirited with the snake intertwining its body around the tortoise while its head confronts the tortoise in an eyeball-to-eyeball fashion.

76

Ling and Zhang Er. During the 1960s and 1970s archaeologists unearthed more than 3, 000 terracotta warriors and other cultural relics from two attendant tombs at Yangjiawan Village in the east part of the Changling Mausoleum. Given this immense size of the two tombs, which were buried with the remains of the celebrated Han-dynasty general Zhou Bo and his son, it is not difficult to imagine how large the collection of burial objects would be in the emperor's own mausoleum.

The Yangling Mausoleum belongs to the remains of Liu Qi, or Emperor Jingdi, the son of Emperor Wendi and Empress Dou. Sitting on the eastern end of the cluster of nine imperial Han tombs at Yuanshang, Yangling is situated at Zhangjiawan Village, Xiajiacun Township in Xianyang's Xindu District. During his fifteen-year reign, Liu Qi carried forward his father's policies and acted on Huang Lao's stratagem of emphasizing cardinal tasks without wasting time and energy on trivial matters and giving the populace the opportunity to build up their economic strengths. As a result he brought about a period of unprecedented peace and prosperity, known in Chinese history as "Piping Times of Peace under Emperors Wendi and Jindi" . When Liu Qi died in 141 BC, his remains were buried in Yangling, to be joined by his wife, Empress Yu, who died fourteen years later. Both tumuli take the shape of an inverted dou with a roughly square base. The emperor's tomb measures thirty-one metres in height and that of his empress, twenty-five metres. An archway is erected on each of the four sides of the mausoleum. In an emergency excavation campaign to make way for the construction of an expressway in 1990, archaeologists discovered a large group of pits buried with terracotta figurines on a total space of 96, 000 square metres. After nearly three years of hectic work, more than 600 painted terracotta figurines and 4,000 cultural relics of all kinds were exhumed from a space of 1, 100 square metres. Statistics show that at least 10,000 terracotta figurines are in the attendant burial pits at the Yangling Mausoleum. As far as art goes, this is undoubtedly an astronomical figure.

The terracotta figurines yielded from Yangling burial pits cover a wide range of imagery, and the warrior image is only one category. All of them are marked by two salient features: first, arms made of wood were attached to the bodies; second, the drapery was neither sculpted nor painted in colour, but made of real fabrics. As the wood and fabrics have long decayed, the figurines appear nude and arm-less, their bodies painted orange-red, chest muscle slightly bulging, bellies smooth and flat and complete with a belly button and penis. They are, in a nutshell, entirely different from Qin and Han terracotta figurines seen else-

77

78

77. A leaping horse — To honour General Huo Qubing's meritorious exploits in combating the Xiongnu nomads, Emperor Wudi had his tomb built in the shape of the Qilian Mountain and decorated it with many large stone sculptures. The dozen stone sculptures which remain to this day are marked for their heroic and monumental imagery; they are a priceless heritage in the treasurehouse of classical Chinese stone sculpture. The horse in this picture, 2.5 metres in length, is on the verge of taking off.

78. A horse overpowering a Xiongnu nomad under its belly — a representative work of the stone sculptures in front of Huo Qibing's tomb. By setting the dashing and debonair image of a horse in sharp contrast with an invader struggling hopelessly for life under the horse's hoofs, the work is meant to say that justice will eventually triumph over evil. Here the rich imagination and unusual artistic ingenuity of the unknown sculptor are brought to best advantage.

79. Reclining Buffalo — A stone sculpture 2.6 by 1.6 metres fashioned out of the natural contours of a boulder. There is something idyllic about the buffalo's calm and reposed image.

80. Reclining Tiger — This stone sculpture in front of Huo Qibing's tomb takes the image of a fierce tiger ready to prance for its prey. Action is entailed in the seemingly tranquil posture of the tiger, looking alert and nimble-limbed, with its body hugging the ground tightly.

79

80

81

82

where. The fact that they are the earliest pottery figurines ever portrayed in the nude in China has rendered them a unique research and artistic value.

Among all the eleven Western-Han imperial mausoleums, Emperor Wudi's Maoling Mausoleum situated at the western end of the mausoleum zone at Nanwei Township, Xingping County, is the largest. History books show that it took fifty-three years to finish this mammoth project. Because the reign of Liu Che, or Emperor Wu, lasted for a long period of time, prior to his death his tomb had already been filled to overflowing with burial objects as a result of the accumulation of yearly entries. Probably out of their admiration for the deceased emperor's monumental achievements in his lifetime, builders heaped the tumulus to an unusual height of 46.5 metres. Over the years hundreds of important cultural relics have been discovered from the Maoling Mausoleum. The bronze horses inlaid with gold, green jade ornaments, bronze rhinoceroses and gold-plated silver incense-burner with a bamboo-shaped handle are all rare and invaluable discoveries from the Maoling Mausoleum, which is surrounded by twenty-odd attendant tombs buried with the remains of Wei Qing, Huo Qubing, Huo Guang and the emperor's other confidantes. The Maoling Museum in front of the Tomb of Huo Qubing is famed for its large collection of sixteen large Han-dynasty stone sculptures which formerly decorated the general's tomb, including stone men, horses, reclining buffalos, prancing tigers, a horse with its hoofs rested on the body of a Xiongnu nomad and a bizarre-looking beast wolfing down a goat. All the sculptures were ingeniously wrought with sparing strokes of the chisel in light of the natural forms of the rocks. Looking vivid and vigorous in crude, simplistic imagery, they are representative of Han-dynasty sculptural art.

81. Gold-plated bronze horse, 62 by 76 cm — Excavated from the eastern side of the Maoling Mausoleum of Emperor Wudi of the Han Dynasty in May 1981. The image of the horse looks steadfast and vigilant with its well-proportioned body standing rod-straight, its neck craning, and its ears erect and taut.

82. Jade door-knocker with an animal-face, 39.2 by 35.6 cm — Unearthed near the Maoling Mausoleum of the Western Han Emperor Wudi in 1974, this is a piece of relief and reticulated jade carving of the face of an animal with glaring eyes and a drooping nose. The four corners of the base plate are carved with the Green Dragon, White Tiger, Scarlet Bird and Black Tortoise. It is the largest Western-Han jade door-knocker so far discovered in China.

83. Gold- and silver-plated bronze incense-burner with a bamboo-shaped handle — Unearthed east of the Maoling Mausoleum of Emperor Wudi of the Western Han Dynasty at Xingping County, this incense-burner stands 58 cm tall with a mountain-like lid and a raised handle in the shape of a bamboo twig. The entire sculpture is plated with gold and silver and two dragons are vividly carved on its pedestal in fluent lines. ▶

In the Mountains: Eighteen Tang Mausoleums

Eighteen emperors of the Tang Dynasty are buried in the northern part of Guanzhong Plain. Chinese feudal society reached its apex during the Tang Dynasty. The consolidation of the centralized monarchy and the abundance of national resources enabled the Tang monarchs to devise a new pattern of imperial tombs by drawing on the predecessors of bygone dynasties. The mausoleums were bigger, and the layout was an imitation of that of the capital city of Chang'an, and hierarchy was more stringently embodied in the arrangement of attendant tombs and the shape and size of decorative stone sculptures. Of the eighteen imperial mausoleums, only four — Xianling, Duanling, Zhuangling and Jingling — feature earth tumuli protruding from the ground. The other fourteen are chamber-caves tunnelled into the middle of a natural mountain, so as to satisfy the emperor's aspiration that even in death he could still rule his country at a commanding position veiled behind a curtain of clouds and surrounded by towering mountains. From a topographical point of view, all the Tang mausoleums are situated at high altitudes so that the deceased could gaze down at the Western-Han imperial tombs in the south in a condescending manner.

The Shaoling Mausoleum, in which the bodies of Li Shimin (Emperor Taizong) and Empress Changsun are buried together, is situated on the Jiujun Mountain to the northeast of Liquan County. Covering an area of 20, 000 hectares 60 kilometres in perimeter, it is the first and the biggest of all the Tang-dynasty mausoleums ever to be built into a mountain, and, what is more, it has the most attendant tombs. History records show that construction of Shaoling lasted thirteen years from 638 AD or the tenth year of the Zhenguan Reign, when Empress Changsun was buried, to the twenty-third year of the Zhenguan Reign with the entombment of the remains of Emperor Taizhong. The Xuangong Palace, or the funeral chamber, was drilled into the middle of the major peak of the Jiujun Mountain, with five stone gates erected on a 250-metre-long passageway. A dazzling array of the emperor's favorite treasures was kept inside. With a "grandeur unseen in the mundane world," as the saying goes, the collection is said to include the masterpiece "Introducing the Orchid Pavilion" in the handwriting of the famous calligrapher Wang Xizi. Ground structures are scattered about the mausoleum, with a sacrificial altar and the Black Tortoise Archway in the north, the Gate of Scarlet Bird and Xiandian Hall in the south, and the Resting Hall in the southwest. The group of stone sculptures placed behind the Black Tortoise Archway is known for its high-relief stone carvings of horses named Saluzi, Telebiao, Qingzhui, Shenhuachi, Horse with Curling Hair and Horse with White Hoofs, all being likenesses of the six steeds Li Shimen had used in his combat years. After he took the throne, he had the horses' images carved into sculptures and placed at both ends of the Black Tortoise Archway along with a stone screen inscribed with the emperor's four-line poem in the handwriting of the famous calligrapher Ouyang Xun. The horse sculptures and the calligraphic work earned a reputation as unprecedented art masterpieces. Two of the horse statues, Saluzi and the Horse with Curling Hair, are found in the Museum of the University of Philadelphia, and the other fours are on display in the Stele Forest Museum of Xi'an.

More than 200 attendant aristocrat tombs are scattered south of Shaoling Mausoleum, and the locations of 185 of them have been verified. A dozen of them have been unearthed, including the tombs of Zheng Rentai, Weichi Jingde, Li Ji, Ashinazhong, Princess Linchuan and Zhang Shigui. Most of the attendant tombs are of considerable sizes to indicate the emperor's high considerations for his imperial family members and major ministers and generals and to embody the motto "The master is noble and his ministers are men of dignity." A wealth of sacrificial objects, including murals, porcelains, stone carvings, bronzes and pottery figurines, have been brought to light from these tombs. All of them are embodiments of the high artistic and

84

cultural attainments of the Tang Dynasty and faithful reflections of the social mosaic of the Tang society.

The Qianling Mausoleum on the Liangshan Mountain in north Xianxian County is smaller than Shaoling but it is relatively better preserved than any other Tang mausoleums. It is the only mausoleum in China buried with two Tang monarchs: Li Zhi, or Gaozong the Third Tang emperor, and Empress Wu. According to New Tang Annals: Biography of Emperor Gaozong, the emperor was buried in Qianling in 684 or the first year of the Guangshe Reign; in 705, or the first year of the Shenlong Reign, Empress Wu died, and her remains were buried with her husband a year later. The mausoleum was tunnelled into the north Peak which is taller than the Liangshan Mountain's other two peaks. Looking like a woman's two breasts, these two shorter peaks form a natural screen for the Qianling Mausoleum. The entire complex consists of two sections. The inner section is surrounded on four sides by walls 1,438-1, 582 metres in circumference, with a gate and three gate-towers in each of the four sides. The gates are flanked by large stone lions but the northern gate is also flanked by stone horses. Other large stone sculptures are found lining both sides of the road in front of the mausoleum, including pairs of huabiao ceremonial columns, the Gate of Scarlet Bird and winged beasts, five pairs of stone men and 61 statues of representatives of ethnic peoples from other parts of the country. This setup of stone sculptures had since become the stereotype for imperial mausoleums of later generations. Moreover, two huge stone tablets are placed at an open space at the Gate of Scarlet Bird. The one to the west is inscribed with the text of Empress Wu's "Tablet Recording the Exploits of the Sacred Emperor" in the handwriting of Emperor Zhongzong. The tablet to the east, known as "Blank Tablet", is carved with eight intertwining dragons. When this tablet was first erected it was carved with nothing but tracery on its four rims; it was left blank either because Empress Wu thought her accomplishment and virtue were so high as to be beyond words, or because the empress maintained that her own merits and dismerits should be left unsaid so that posterity could free free to comment. Thus for its wordlessness this tablet gained an uncanny reputation.

Archaeologists discovered that, in conformity with the historical record that the "stone passageway to the burial chamber was fortified with metallurgical work", the passageway into Qianling Mausoleum was paved with quarried stone slabs joined with iron bars, with the seams sealed with molten iron. So far no traces of tomb robbery have been found, a fact which indicates that Qianling is the best preserved Tang-dynasty necropolis. Since 1960, seventeen attendant tombs have been unearthed at Qianling, including the tombs of Princess Yongtai, Prince Zhanghuai, and Prince Yide. A total of 4,000 precious artifacts have been found. In the 1970s, the Qianling Museum was established in the compound of Princess Yongtai's tomb. A visit to this museum never fails to inspire a nostalgic feeling for the great Tang Dynasty's cultural achievements.

85

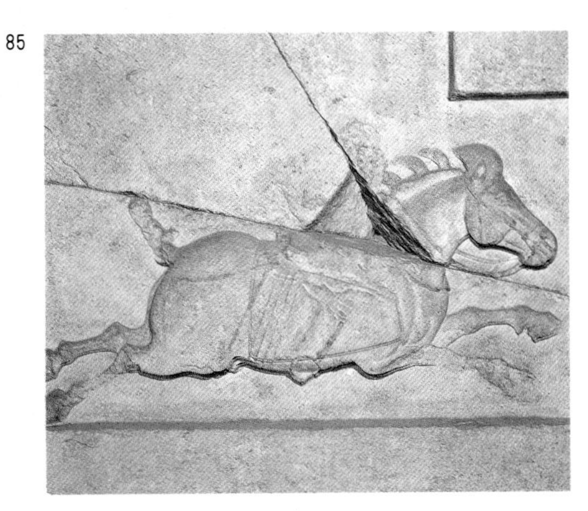

86

87

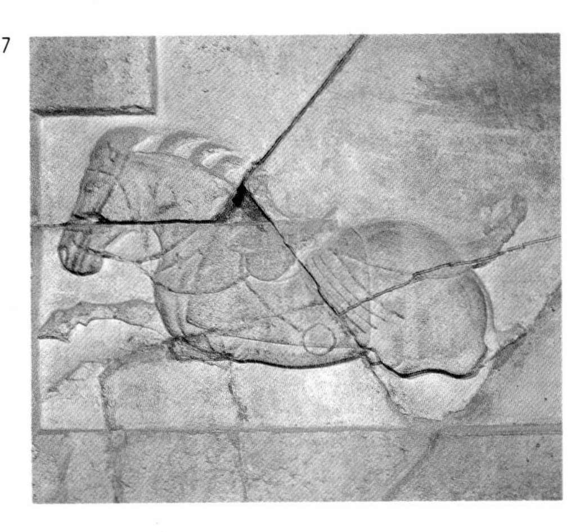

◀ **84**. Passageway in the tomb of Princess Changle — Princess Changle was the fifth daughter of Li Shimin, or the Tang Emperor Taizong. After her death she was buried in the Shaoling Mausoleum in Yanxia Township, Liquan County. A 1986 excavation yielded more than a hundred burial objects from the tomb. Four murals of carriages and horses and ceremonial processions were found on the eastern and western walls of the passageway.

85. Horse with White Hoofs, one of the six stone horses at Shaoling.

86. Telebiao, one of the six stone horses at Shaoling.

87. Shenfachi, one of the six stone horses at Shaoling.

88

89

88. Qingzhui, one of the six stone horses at Shaoling.
89. Stone animals standing in front of a tomb at Shuangtou Town. ▶

90

91

92

93

90. Winged Horse at the Tailing mausoleum.
91. Squatting stone lion at the Tailing Mausoleum.
92. Walking lion at the Shunling Mausoleum — The Shunling Mausoleum situated north of Xianyang is the tomb of Lady Yang, mother of Empress Wu. To show off her power and position, the empress had huge stone sculptures placed by the Shunling Mausoleum, and the walking lion is one of them. Standing 2.5 metres tall, the lion is depicted in a walking position, with its head raised high in a most awesome fashion.
93. Unicorn at Shunling Mausoleum — The unicorn, also known as Tianlu, has a head like that of a deer, hoofs like those of a horse and a body like that of a cattle, and its wings are graced with cloud-like tracery. Its tail droops to link with the stone pedestal. The space under its belly is large enough to seat a number of people. This is regarded as a fine example of all the stone sculptures of the Shunling Mausoleum.

94. Stone man at Qiaoling Mausoleum — Ten pairs of 2.2-metre-tall stone men are found in front of the Qiaoling Mausoleum of Li Dan or Emperor Ruizong. They wear dragon crowns and loose-fitting robes with long sword in hand, standing deviously with wide faces, long beards and round eyes.
95. Stone tiger at the Xianling Mausoleum — There are four pairs of such stone tigers around the Xianling Mausoleum of Emperor Gaozu situated in Xumu Township, Sanyuan County. The tigers are depicted in a heroic posture with alert eyes and sinewy legs.
96. Winged horse at the Chongling Mausoleum.

96 ▶

94

95

97

98

97. Group stone sculptures at Qiaoling Mausoleum.
98. The blank stone tablet.
99. The Qianling Mausoleum.
100. Painted terracotta sculpture of a horseback-riding figurine.
101. Passageway in Prince Yongtai's tomb — Prince Yongtai, whose name was Li Xianhui, was the grand-daughter of Emperor Gaozong and Empress Wu; after her death she was buried in the Qianling Mausoleum. During an excavation campaign in 1960, archaeologists discovered large numbers of burial objects from the tomb. Murals were found on the walls of the passageway and the tomb chamber; executed exquisitely with bright colours, clear-cut lines and rich contents, they are a precious heritage in ancient Chinese painting.

99

100

101

102. Tri-coloured utensil — A utensil glazed in low temperature, it is marked for its multifarious colours. The tri-coloured utensils unearthed from the attendant tombs of the Qianling Mausoleum are among the best of high-Tang cultural relics. The tri-coloured bowls are graced with white- and green-glazed belts in an ingenious way.

104. Painted terracotta sculpture of a mounted man wearing a straw hat.

102

104

103

103. Painted pottery figurines of civilian official and military officer.

A Map of Geogrpahical Distribution of Major Imperial Tombs in Xi'an Area

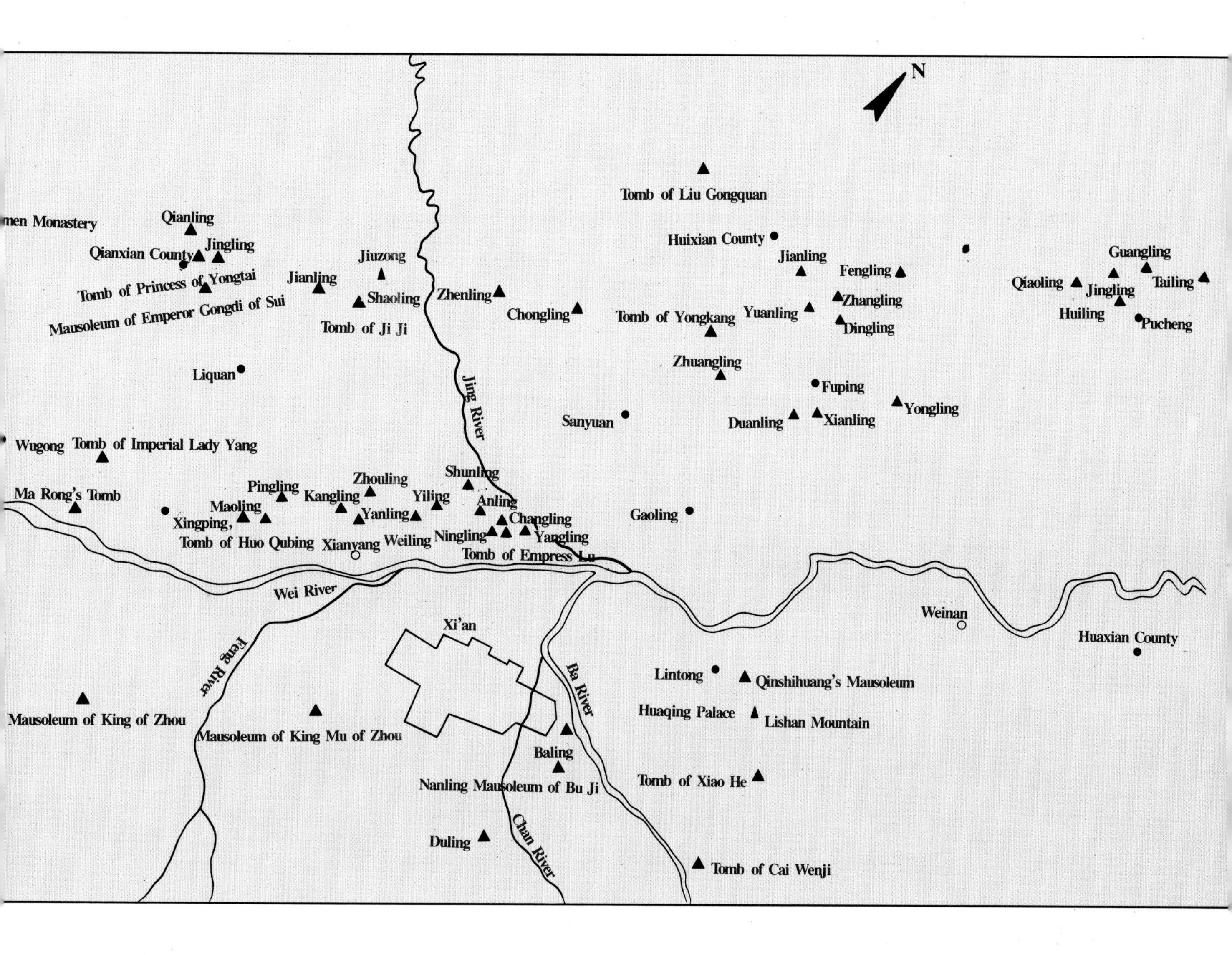

Where Deities Meet: Famous Temples

The ancient city of Chang'an was, for a considerably long period of time, a political and economic centre as well as a religious sanctuary. Religion reached its acme during the Tang dynasty thanks to political stability and a robust economy. Not only was the indigenous Taoism disseminated far and wide, foreign religions, too, made much headway in social life.

Since Buddhism was spread into China during the Han Dynasty, it had provided the code of thinking for many generations of Chinese aristocrats, particularly during the Southern and Northern Dynasties. By the Tang Dynasty, respecting and worshipping the Buddha had become the order of the day. Chang'an, an international metropolis sitting at the eastern end of the Euroasian Silk Road, became a gathering place for famous priests and monks of all manners of religion. Its many pagodas and monasteries were thronged with worshipers listening eagerly to some high monks' preaching. According to historical documents, for a time there were as many as 122 monasteries and 31 nunneries in Chang'an. Emperors and aristocrats alike took great pride in building monasteries and loved to be consecrated by having holy water sprinkled on their heads. Some monasteries had grown to unbelievable sizes. The Ci'en Monastery, for instance, boasted a total of 1897 rooms in a dozen courtyards of pavilions, halls and chambers which covered a total area of 400 mu. Even more grandiose was the Zhangyun Monastery outside the east city gate, which had 4,130-odd rooms in forty-eight compounds, the result of the "toil of one hundred million labourers", as a history book puts it. Not only the various sects of Buddhism and Taoism (the state religion) were active in the highly civilized and extraverted Tang society, but such foreign religions as Zoroastrianism, Nestorianism, Manichaeism and Islamism also found their way into China. Religion played an indispensable role in cultural exchanges between China and foreign countries.

Even today, many sites of religious and cultural interest are still around in and out of Chang'an. The towering Greater Wild-Goose Pagoda in the Ci'en Monastery and the statuesque Lesser Wild-Goose Pagoda in the Jianfu Monastery, have become the twin emblems of the famous historical and cultural city of Xi'an. The Famen Monastery regained its position as a Buddhist sanctuary with the discovery of a Tang-dynasty collection of four sariras which are attributed to Sakyamuni. Other famous religious establishments, such as the Great Xinshan Monastery, the Qinglong Temple and the Xiangji Temple, have become famous tourist attractions and sites for Sino-foreign friendly exchanges. The Baxian (Eight Immortals) and Shuilu (Water-and-Land) temples are famous Taoist sanctuaries, while the Great Muslim Mosque stands both as a rare architecture phenomenon and a major centre for Islamism.

Caotang Temple

The Caotang Temple, where Kumarajiva, a high monk from the West Territory, preached on Buddhist doctrines, is situated in Huxian County thirty kilometres southwest of Xi'an. The temple nestles against the foot of the Zhongnan Mountain on the eastern bank of the Feng river in a setting both picture-perfect and peaceful. It is known for one of the "Eight Sights of Chang'an" , a "smoking well" with whitish vapour wafting continuously from its depth.

In the compound stands a 2. 3-metre-tall, 12-layered stupa, in which the sariars of Kumarajiva are enshrined. An octagonal structure fashioned out of marble of different hues in each layer, the stupa is also called "Eight-Treasure Marble Stupa" , whose top and pedestal are encrusted with elaborate tracery. The twenty-odd stone tablets in the temple are important materials for the study of the monastic organization and Buddhist history of various dynasties. The stone tablet dedicated to the priest Dinghui was inscribed in 855 AD or the ninth year of the Dazhong Reign of the Tang Dynasty in a calligraphic style that is elegant and lovable; Liu Gongquan, the celebrated mid-Tang calligrapher, left his seal-script signature on the tablet.

105

106

105. A wooden sculpture of Kumarajiva.

106. The stupa enshrined with the sariars of Kumarajiva (344-413 AD).

Famen Monastery

The Famen Monastery, extolled as the "forefather of all all monasteries and temples in Guangzhong Plain" , is situated at Famen Town, Fufeng County, 120 kilometres west of Chang'an.

The monastery rose to fame as an imperial religious establishment when the Tang court conferred the title "State-Protected Sariars of Sakyamuni" on a collection of sariars enshrined under a stupa in the compound. At the time as many as five thousand monks lived in the monastery's twenty-four compounds. The sariars were taken out for public display once in every thirty years. During the Tang Dynasty, the underground palace beneath the stupa was opened and closed on seven occasions, and Sakyamuni's sariars were escorted to and from the imperial court seven times in unprecedented throng and pomp.

In 1985 the Ming-dynasty brick pagoda in the Famen Monastery collapsed. From the debris archaeologists uncovered the Tang-dynasty underground palace which lay one metre below the ground, and they made archaeology history by bringing to light the four sariars which had been repeatedly escorted to the Tang imperial court along with large amounts of treasures offered as sacrificial objects, including gold and silver vessels, porcelains, glassware, pearls and precious stones and silks.

The sariars enshrined in the Famen Monastery's underground palace are contained in a box made of multiple layers of gold, silver, crystal, jade, pearls and sandalwood. After they were unearthed they have been placed back into the newly refurbished underground palace. When these sariars were first spotted, they were lying in the midst of a thick pile of cultural relics — 121 gold and silver vessels, eight bronze vessels, twenty pieces of glassware, 19 porcelains, 11 stone carvings, 400-odd pearls and pieces of jade, and hundreds of silk fabrics. The gold and silver vessels include daily utensils, sacrificial vessels and musical instruments used in religious ceremonies; the designs and shapes of some of them were seen for the first time among Tang-dynasty artifacts. All these gold and silver vessels had been used in the imperial court or were made specially for enshrining Sakyamuni's sariars; marked by exquisite craftsmanship, each and every one of them is a priceless treasure. The porcelains were also for imperial use, glazed with what is called "smoky colours" , and experts regard them as standards for the study of "smoky-coloured" porcelains. The glassware bears a distinctive cultural style of central and west Asia. Unfortunately, many of the seven hundred pieces of silk fabrics had decayed and become mere ashes. All these objects, which were presented by emperors Yizhong and Xizong and Empress Anhuang during the late Tang Dynasty, have provided significant information for the study of Tang-dynasty politics, economics, culture, religion and exchanges with the rest of the world.

After the excavation of the Famen Monastery was finished, the provincial authorities rebuilt the Ming-dynasty brick stupa and the underground palace below it and established the Famenshi Museum. All the national treasures uncovered from the underground palace are now kept in the museum's Chamber of Treasures in an effort to restore the monastery to its Tang-dynasty glory and turn it into a major Buddhist establishment and tourist attraction.

107

109

107. Four sariras of Sakyamuni's finger bone were unearthed from the Tang-dynasty underground palace of the Famen Monastery in Fufeng County in 1987. The first, second and fourth sariars are known as "shadowy bone"; and the third sarira, featuring a whitish cuter crust, with its dark-yellow inner crust dotted with black spots, is regarded as the Buddha's spirit-bone, or his Dharmakaya sarira. During the Tang Dynasty, these sariras were objects of worship for officials and commoners alike. They had been preserved in the underground palace of the Famen Monastery after it was closed in 874 Ad, or the 15th year of the Xiantong Reign of the Tang Dynasty. Today, they are still kept in the underground palace.

108. Famen Monastery.

109. Gold-plated silver incense-burner in the shape of a turtle, with its five legs graced with lotus-flower patterns — Unearthed from the Tang-dynasty underground palace of the Famen Monastery in Fufeng County in 1987, this incense-burner stands 29.5 cm tall and weighs 6,408 grammes, and is composed of a five-legged burner and a pedestal. Forty-nine characters are inscribed on it to indicate that it was made in the imperial workshop of the Tang Dynasty.

Ci'en Monastery

110. A Buddhist scripture written during the Tang Dynasty.
111. The Greater Wild-Goose Pagoda. ▶

The Ci'en Monastery was named Wulou Monastery when it was first established during the Sui Dynasty. In 648 AD, or the twenty-second year of the Guanzhen Reign, Prince Li Zhi (who later became Emperor Gaozong) changed the name of the monastery into Ci'en (meaning, Her Majesty's Motherly Kindness) in memory of his mother Empress Wende. The monastery is a colossal affair with 1,897 halls and pavilions arranged in a dozen or so courtyards on an area of four hundred mu. The pagoda erected in the same time as the monastery itself used to be a five-layered 180-metre-high structure in the shape of an Indian pagoda, but not long after its completion it began to slant. During the Changan Reign (701-704) of Empress Wu, the imperial court rebuilt the pagoda which we see today, a four-sided, seven-layered structure standing 64 metres high in the southeast part of the ancient city of Chang'an and facing the Zhongnan Mountain in the distance.

During his stint as abbot of the Ci'en Monastery in its early days, the celebrated Tang-dynasty monk Xuan Zang (Tripitaka) dedicated himself to construction and expansion work while presiding over the monastery's general affairs. The Greater Wild-Goose Pagoda was actually built for the purpose of storing the Buddhist manuscripts he had fetched from India. Xuan Zang, a great Buddhist theoretician, translator and traveller in Chinese history, started his solitary India-bound journey from Chang'an in 628 AD, or the second year of the Guanzhen Reign, in search of Buddhist scriptures. Overcoming untold hardships along the Silk Road, he eventually arrived at his destination seventeen years later. After he returned to China, he established a large translation centre in the Ci'en Monastery. The team of prestigious monks he had enrolled from all over the country accomplished an unprecedented feat by translating into Chinese seventy-four Buddhist scriptures in 1,335 volumes. In the process of compiling and translating Buddhist scriptures he established the Buddhist discipline of learning known as Aspects of Things, and the Ce'en Monastery became the cradle for it. Xuan Zang's foreign disciples brought his theories back to Korea and Japan, where he became an internationally renowned master. His travelogue Buddhist Records of the Western World in the Tang Dynasty remains to this day as an important classic with a high academic value.

The Ci'en Monastery is located close to the Qujiang Pond, a well-known tourist resort in Xi'an. The lofty Greater Wild-Goose Pagoda and the beautiful Qujiang Pond set off each other to form a wonderful picture in the capital of the great Tang empire. In those years men of letters often dined at the monastery and gathered at the foot of the pagoda to write inscriptions in eulogy of nobility and meritorious deeds.

Today, after so many years of ups and downs Ci'en Monastery remains a popular sanctuary for worshipers.

110

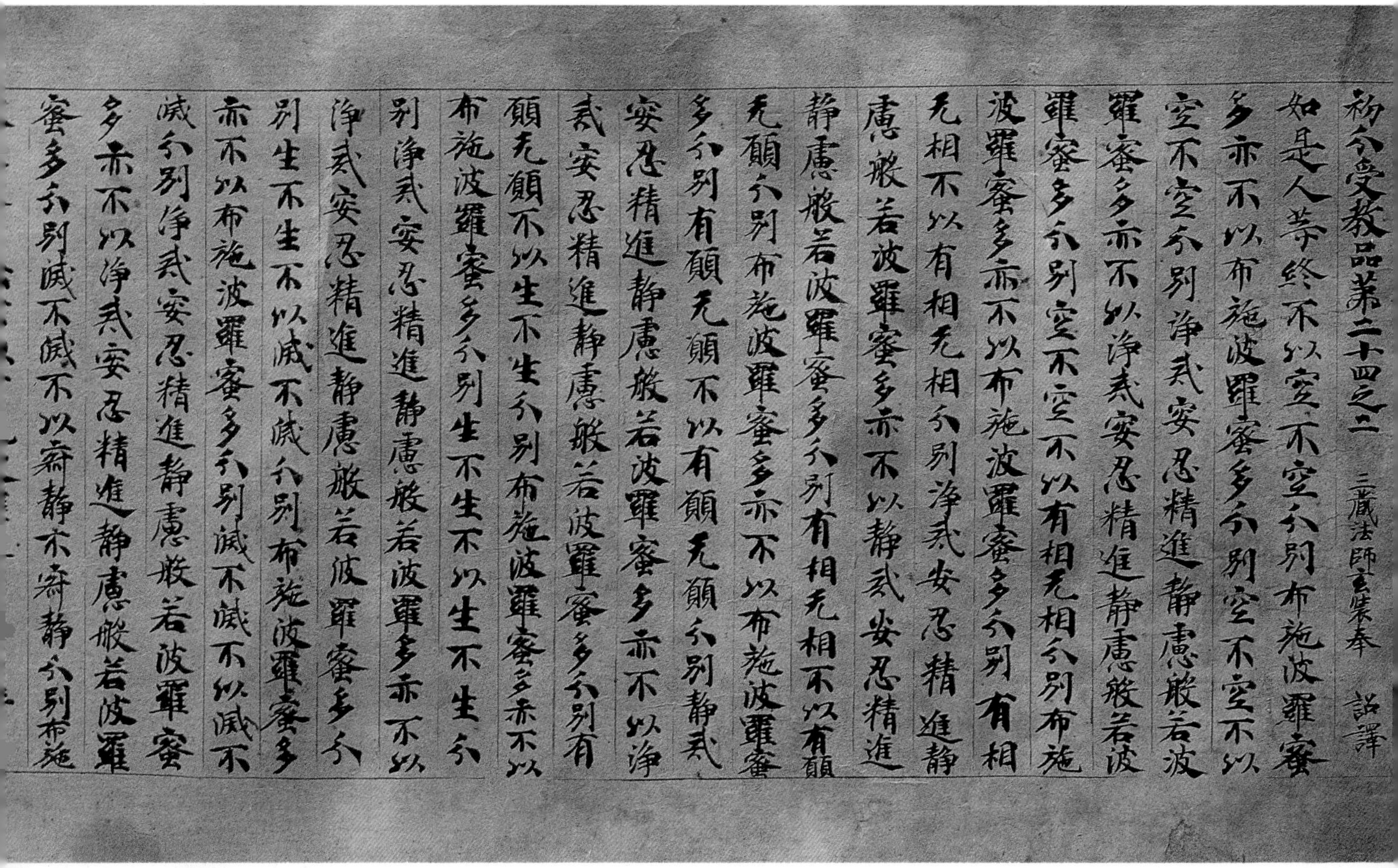
初分受教品第二十四之二　三藏法師玄奘奉　詔譯
如是人等終不以空不空分別布施波羅蜜
多亦不以布施波羅蜜多分別空不空不以
空不空分別淨戒安忍精進靜慮般若波
羅蜜多亦不以淨戒安忍精進靜慮般若波
羅蜜多分別空不空不以有相无相分別布施
波羅蜜多亦不以布施波羅蜜多分別有相
无相不以有相无相分別淨戒安忍精進靜
慮般若波羅蜜多亦不以靜戒安忍精進
靜慮般若波羅蜜多分別有相无相不以有願
无願分別布施波羅蜜多亦不以布施波羅蜜
多分別有願无願不以有願无願分別靜戒
安忍精進靜慮般若波羅蜜多亦不以淨
戒安忍精進靜慮般若波羅蜜多分別有
願无願不以生不生分別布施波羅蜜多亦不以
布施波羅蜜多分別生不生不以生不生分
別淨戒安忍精進靜慮般若波羅蜜多亦不以
淨戒安忍精進靜慮般若波羅蜜多分
別生不生不以滅不滅分別布施波羅蜜多
亦不以布施波羅蜜多分別滅不滅不以滅不
滅分別淨戒安忍精進靜慮般若波羅蜜
多亦不以淨戒安忍精進靜慮般若波羅
蜜多分別滅不滅不以寂靜不寂靜分別布施

Great Xingshan Temple

The Great Xingshan Temple is located on the southern outskirts of Xi'an. Historical records show that the temple was first established in the Tang-dynasty capital of Chang'an during the 256-289 AD period from the Taishi to Taikang Reigns of Emperor Wudi of the Western Jin Dynasty, and was expanded during the Northern Zhou Dynasty. When the Sui Dynasty built its capital city of Daxing, the temple was moved to Jingshanfang and renamed Great Xingshan Temple. During the Sui and Tang dynasties it became the most popular Buddhist establishment in the capital city.

The Great Xingshan Temple was one of three major centres in Chang'an for the translation of Buddhist scriptures into Chinese; it was also the cradle of Tantrism (or esoteric Buddhism) in China. Famous Indian monks Subhakasimha (637-735 AD) had stayed in the temple and lectured on tantric doctrines. Amoghavajra (705-774 AD), who had extensively studied tantric canons in India, later became chief translator at the Great Xingshan Temple, where he translated more than five hundred Buddhist scriptures, presided over the consecration ceremony for the Tang emperor, and studied Sanskrit Buddhist scriptures collected from other monasteries and temples around the capital city, thereby making indelible contributions to the compilation and research of canonical Buddhist writings and disseminating Buddhist doctrines. During the reign of Emperor Daizong, he was decorated as Commander with Unequalled Honour, Duke Su of State, and Chancellor of the National Academy; after his death the imperial court conferred the posthumously title "Monk Amoghavajra of Great Truth, Extensive Wisdom and Tripitaka", and earmarked ten thousand strings of money for the construction of the Stupa of Amoghavajra's Sariras. A stone tablet inscribed with five Chinese characters written by Xu Hao is now kept in the Stele Forest of Xi'an; the seven characters read, "Stele in Memory of His Highness Monk Amoghavajra". Most of the structures in existence in the temple were built during the Ming Dynasty. The complex is flanked on the east and west sides by the Bell and Drum towers. The front door opens to the Vajra Hall, behind which stands the Grand Hall dedicated to a statue of Sakyamuni. Erected on both sides of the the Hall of Avalokitesvara (Goddess of Mercy) with a Thousand Hands and a Thousand Eyes behind the Grand Hall are two Five-Pillared Transepts. A horizontal plaque inscribed with the message "Enlightening the Multitude" written by Qing Emperor Guangxu is hung above the frontal gate of the Hall of Dharma in the rear courtyard. The Tang-dynasty Spinning Wheel and Tripitaka Pavilion now lies in a roughly square pile of ruins one metres high. In 1995, members of the Japanese tantric Shingon-shu Sect erected a bronze statue of Kstigarbha (Guardian of the Earth) in front of the ruins in memory of the cradle of their sect and the friendship between the Chinese and Japanese people. The Great Xingshan Temple is not only a Buddhist sanctuary but also an excellent tourist attraction. Clusters of ancient cypress trees soar up into the sky and heap up dense foliage, shutting the temple off the sky and the sun and the boisterous city life, and rendering a quality of sequestered peace to the entire compound.

112. Mountain archway.
113. A religious ceremony.

112

113

Jianfu Temple

"Morning Bell Toll at the Goose Pagoda" , which is one of the eight sights in the ancient capital city of Chang'an, refers to the sound of bell from the Lesser Wild-Goose Pagoda which stands in the Jianfu Temple in the southern suburb of Xi'an and faces the Greater Wild-Goose Pagoda in the distance. For the last thousand years, the reverberating toll of the bell near the Lesser Wild-Goose Pagoda has been regarded as the harbinger of dawn in this ancient city.

For a time the largest monastery in Chang'an, the Jianfu Temple was first built in 684 AD or the first year of the Wenming Reign of the Tang Dynasty in honour of Li Zhi, or Emperor Gaozong. Its original name was Xianfu Temple. Yijing (635-713 AD), a high monk of the Tang Dynasty, chaired an organization in this temple for the translation of Buddhist scriptures. He left Chang'an in 671 AD or the second year of Xianheng Reign, sailed on board a Persian ship across the sea to Indonesia and India, where he visited famous temples and monasteries. Twenty-five years later, having toured more than thirty countries, he returned with more than four hundred Buddhist scriptures, to the warm welcome of Empress Wu. Back in the capital city, Yijing enrolled accomplished monks from India and West Territory to render Buddhist canons into Chinese and compile and write books, thereby making major contributions to the research of religious literature and the history and culture of China and foreign countries.

The Lesser Wild-Goose Pagoda was first built during the Jinglong Reign (707-709 AD) of Emperor Zhongzong to store the scriptures and Buddhist statues brought back by Yijing. The pagoda with its folded eaves stands 43 metres high in 15 layers and its door lintels are decorated with finely crafted tracery. An earthquake during the Tang Dynasty resulted in a vertical crack in the pagoda. For a time the crack was used as a sign for predicting the year's harvest: when the crack closed, it meant good weather for the crops; and when the crack widened it entailed dry spell and crop failure in the offing.

The large cast-iron bell hanging in the bell tower of the monastery was cast in 1192, or the third year of the Mingchang Reign of the Jin Dynasty. It is of an unusual size, 3.5 metres in height and 2.7 metres in diameter, and weighing more than 10,000 kilogrammes.

All the buildings in the Jianfu Temple were built during the Ming Dynasty except the pagoda which dates back to the Tang Dynasty. As an imperial religious establishment, the temple survived Emperor Wuzong's campaign to eliminate Buddhism, but it was burned down in the late Tang Dynasty. Rebuilt during the Song, Yuan and Ming dynasties, it gradually grew to what it is today. After the founding of the People's Republic, the pagoda was buttressed and the crack sealed. However, the pagoda has remained topless over the last five centuries, for architects are still racking their brains for its most authentic design.

114. Ci's Chamber of the Jianfu Monastery.

115 Xia Yanta

Qinglong Monastery

In sunset I mounted the peak
Whose contours accounts for the temple's good name.
With autumn leaves dyeing the cloisters scarlet red,
The verdant mountain is an ideal abode for
the Bud- dha.

These lines are quoted from "Ode to Qinglong Monastery", a poem written by the Tang-dynasty poet Zhu Qingyu. The Qinglong Monastery is situated at Yuanshang in the southeast part of the Tang-dynasty capital of Chang'an. The place got a name for itself because of the monastery, and the monastery rose to fame partly because of the name of the place. During the Tang Dynasty this place was a renowned scenic spot, and the Qinglong Monastery was a prestigious monastery of considerable size.

The ruins of the Tang-dynasty Qinglong Monastery are found north of Tielumiao Village on the southeast outskirts of Xi'an. The temple was first built in 582, or the second year of the Kaihuang Reign of Emperor Wendi of the Sui Dynasty. Previously it was known as Ganlinggan Monastery. During the Dalie Reign (766-780 AD) of the Tang Dynasty, many high monks from China and other parts of the world came to this monastery for lectures on tantric Buddhism given by abbot Huiguo (752-805 AD). Thus the Qinglong Monastery became a major centre for the dissemination of the doctrines of Tantrism.

During his stay in Chang'an the Japanese monk Kukai (774-835 AD) had the opportunity to be enlightened by abbot Huiguo. Kukai returned to Japan as a fastidious student of the tantric culture and a well-accomplished Sinologist; with a large shipload of Buddhist classics and other books he had brought from China, he established the Japanese tantric Shingon-shu sect and set up an altar to propagate tantric doctrines, thereby becoming one of the few highly accomplished Japanese monks schooled in a Tang-dynasty religious establishment. Members of the Eight Eminent Japanese Studying in Tang, such as Enchin (815-891 AD) and Enzin (793-864), had all studied at the Qinglong Monastery and did their bit for Sino-Japanese friendship.

Since the early 1960s, the Archaeology Institute of the Chinese Academy of Sciences has conducted partial excavations of the ruins of the Tang-dynasty Qinglong Monastery and brought to light the foundations of three halls and the square pedestal for a wooden pagoda, along with a gold-inlaid bronze stupa of the Buddha, a silver Buddhist statue, the fragmented pedestal for a tri-coloured Buddhist sculpture, and such building materials as tiles, semitubular tiles, tile-ends with lotus-flower patterns and bricks carved with lotus-flower patterns.

116. The memorial hall of Huiguo and Kukai.

Xiangji Monastery

The Xiangji Monastery, situated seventeen kilometres to the southwest of Xi'an at Xiangji Village in Chang'an County's Shenhe Tableland, is the cradle of the Ching-tu (Pure Land) Sect of Chinese Buddhism.

It was built by the monk Huaihui in 706, or the second year of the Shenlong Reign of the Tang emperor Zhongzong, in memory of his tutor Shandao (613-681 AD). In his poem "Passing by Xiangji Temple" the celebrated Tang-dynasty poet Wan Wei wrote:

In the cloud-enveloped mountains
Stretching for many a mile
Sprawls the unknown Xiangji Temple.
Out of nowhere in the depth of the mountain,
Blanketed by track-less ancient wood,
Comes the toll of a bell,
While the gurgling springs are
muffled by truculent rocks.

These lines give perfect expression to the sequestered repose of a monastery kept away from the boisterous city life. The Xiangji Monastery, indeed, was an ideal place for Buddhists seeking to cultivate virtue in seclusion.

Shandao was a major master of the Ching-tu Sect who rose to fame after the emperor had appointed him to supervise the construction of a giant statue of Losana to be enshrined in the Fengxian Temple at Longmen, Luoyang. He copied the Amitabhasutra in hundreds of thousands of volumes and painted three hundred murals which are pictorial stories about his sect. Thanks to his unremitting efforts, the Ching-tu became the most populous and influential Buddhist sect in China. After the sect spread into Japan, it struck roots and prospered as well.

The Great Hall, the Vajra Hall, the Monks' Dormitory and other structures existing in the Xiangji Monastery were all built in recent times. The Shandao Pagoda, the only extant Tang-dynasty structure in the compound, bears close resemblance to the Lesser Wild-Goose Pagoda. At a height of thirty-three metres, with only eleven layers now in existence, this pagoda is a unique combination of folded eaves and pavilion styles. Of the monastery's tiny stupas, only a five-layered brick structure enshrined with the remains of the Tang-dynasty monk Wanhui remains intact.

In 1980, Buddhists from China and Japan held a summons ceremony at the Xiangji Monastery to commemorate the passing away of Master Shandao. A sculpture of the master is placed in the newly-built Great hall as a gift from Japanese monks. The Xiangji Monastery is not only the mecca for the Ching-tu Sect, but also an emblem of Sino-Japanese friendship.

117. Master Shandao's gold-plated wooden sculpture.
118. The stupa of Shandao (613-681 AD).

118

117

Xingjiao Temple

Twenty kilometres south of Xi'an lies the Shaoling Tableland, also known as Fanchuan during the Tang Dynasty, which is a picturesque place strewn with rich families' mansions and Buddhist temples. The Xingjiao Temple (Temple for Promoting Buddhism) is one of the eight major Buddhist institutions there. After the famous monk Xuan Zang passed away, his remains were buried at White Deer Tableland on the eastern bank of the Chan River. When Li Zhi, or Emperor Gaozong, had his tomb moved to Shaoling Tableland, a monastery and a pagoda were built in memory of this great Buddhist master. After the monastery was completed it was named "Great Tang Temple for Protecting the Country and Promoting Buddhism".

The Xingjiao Temple suffered repeated damages in war and was rebuilt in various dynastic periods. Today, three brick pagodas are still there along with a mountain archway, bell and drum towers, the great hall and the dharma hall. In the courtyard west of the main hall stands a Tripitaka chamber which houses a Ming and Qing collection of a thousand volumes of Buddhist scriptures, Pali scriptures inscribed on palm leaves from Borassus flabelliformis, and a white marble statue of Maitreya from Myanmar (Burma). The main hall is enshrined with a statue of Sakyamuni, and its walls are graced with stone inscriptions of the full text of the Vajracchedikapra-jnaparamitasutra. Three pagodas are situated in the Ce'en Pagoda Courtyard on the west side; one of them, under which the remains of Xuan Zang were buried, is a four-sided five-layered brick a la wooden structure twenty-three metres in height, which is unique in architecture history. The "Epitaph in Honour of the Tang Tripitaka and Master Bianjue" inscribed on the pagoda relates the life and accomplishments of Xuan Zang; the pagoda is flanked on both sides by two smaller brick pagodas seven metres high and in three layers, which were reliquaries for Tripitaka's two disciples Kuiji and Yuance, the former being the nephew of the famous minister Weichi Jingde of the early Tang Dynasty and the latter a monk from Korea.

After Xuan Zang's death, his remains were buried in a gold coffin encased in an silver outer coffin, but shortly after his burial the coffins were robbed. Since then the master's sariras and burial objects have been missing. In 1943, invading Japanese troops at Zhonghua Gate, Nanjing, unearthed a stone box containing Xuan Zang's skullcap; the inscriptions on the box say that after the monk Kezheng came into possession of the skullcap, he brought it to Nanjing in 1027 or the fifth year of the Tianshen Reign of the Song Dynasty. Its reappearance in another place was indeed miraculous.

119. Pali Buddhist scripture written on palm leaves of the Borassus flabelliformis.
120. Xuan Zang's stupa.

119

120

Shuilu Temple

121. An overview from the Pavilion-Watching Terrace.
122. The terrace where Buddhist scriptures were interpreted by some high monks.

The Shuilu Temple (Temple of Water and Land), skirted by sparkling rivers at the foot of the Qinling Mountain fifty kilometres southeast of Xi'an, is famed for its extensive collection of finely crafted and colourfully painted relief sculptures on its walls.

Behind the mountain archway of the temple stand the Frontal hall, Central hall, the Hall of Mahavira and other structures, most of them built during the Ming and Qing dynasties, although the temple itself was established during the Tang Dynasty or the Southern and Northern Dynasties. The structures that can be seen today were built with money provided by Zhu Huai, Prince Qin of the Ming Dynasty, behind the Prayer Hall which had served as his mansion.

The dazzling array of painted relief sculptures can be seen in four sections: the south and north gables, the western partition wall, and the western peripheral wall of the Great Hall. But those on the south and north gables are the most spectacular. The relief sculptures, arranged from south to north in several layers, form a pictorial storybook about the life of Sakyamuni. The images include various Buddhas, bodhisattvas, flying apsaras and alms-providers as well as dragons, phoenixes, lions, elephants, cattle and unicorns, set in gardens, pavilions and chambers, on mountainsides and in the rivers. Each figure is depicted in vivid imagery with a distinct personality. The Buddha always appears as a paragon of benevolence, the bodhisattvas look handsome, and the alms-providers look humble and pious. Coloration is bright and variegated, and the artistic appeal is rather enchanting.

So numerous are the figures in this huge collection of relief sculptures that so far nobody has succeeded to give an accurate "body count". As a local saying goes, there are as many figures, birds, animals, flowers and trees as "three hectolitres and six decalitres of vegetable seeds". The Shuilu Temple is not only a sacred religious sanctuary but also a treasurehouse of painted sculpture.

122

Louguan Terrace

Grand Master Yin Xi, who was also commander of Hangu Pass during the Zhou Dynasty, had a thatched pavilion built at the foot of a southwest mountain in Xi'an so that he could observe the movement of the celestial body. One day, amidst an auspicious puff of violet cloud drifted from the east, the great philosopher Lao Zi arrived. Yin Xi, in sheer delight, ushered the great master into his thatched pavilion, where the latter wrote his celebrated Tao Te Jing and had a terrace built on which he delivered lectures. Posterity named it Louguan Terrace, or "Pavilion-Watching Terrace".

The Louguan Terrace is situated at the town of the same name fifteen kilometres southeast of Zhouzhi County. Tucked away amidst a dense riverside bamboo grove at the foot of a mountain, the place with its lovable scenery is a major tourist resort in Guanzhong Plain. Legend has it that King Mu of Zhou, Qinshihuang, Emperor Wu of Han and Emperor Wen of Sui had all built imperial palaces there, which they frequently visited to pray to the god for longevity.

But it was not until the Tang Dynasty that the Louguan Terrace really flourished. Regarding Lao Zi, father of Taoism, as his ancestor, Lu Yuan, the founding emperor of the Tang Dynasty, renamed the Louguan Terrace "Holy Ancestral Palace". During the reign of Li Longji, or Emperor Xuanzong of the Tang Dynasty, more halls were added to the premises, and the name was changed to "Holy Ancestral Temple". Having been repeatedly refurbished during the Song, Yuan, Ming and Qing dynasties, the Louguan Terrace rose to fame as a Taoist sanctum. Famous men of letters and scholars, including Ouyang Xun, Wang Wei and Li Bai of the Tang Dynasty, Mi Fu of the Song Dynasty and Zhao Mengfu of the Yuan Dynasty, visited this place to marvel at the sights and compose poetry and inscribe stone tablets with calligraphic masterpieces.

Most of the existing structures were built during the Ming and Qing dynasties. A narrow footpath conducts through a bamboo grove to the mountain archway, where a collection of stone inscriptions since the Tang Dynasty is situated. Most famous of these is the inscription of the text of "My Impressions on the Holy Ancestral Temple" written in the official script in a calligraphic style which is elegant in a classic way. One of the two hexagonal pavilions in the courtyard houses a stele inscribed with Zhao Mengfu's writing "Pond of Superior Virtue"; the pond, which used to lie between the two pavilions, is no more. The stairway which winds its way from the floor of the inner court up to the top of the terrace is carved into a vertical rock face inscribed with poetic lines composed by men of letters of various dynasties. On the terrace stands the Temple of Lao Zi, looking awe-inspiring as it stands in between four steles carved with the full text of the masterpiece Tao Te Jing. Other buildings on the terrace include the frontal hall, flank halls and transepts.

123. Wall sculptures in the Shuilu Temple.

Great Muslim Mosque

There are a number of Islamic mosques in Xi'an, but the Great Muslim Mosque at Huajue Lane is the largest. It is also one of the two earliest Islamic institutions in the city, the other being at Daxuexi Lane. The two are paired up as the Great East Mosque and the Great West Mosque.

With its front gate facing the east, the Great Muslim Mosque at Huajue Lane measures 50 metres south to north and 250 metres east to west, covering a total area of 12,500 square metres. Known as the best preserved group of Ming-dynasty architecture, the various buildings of the Great Muslim Mosque are providently arranged on a grand scale in four courtyards arrayed from east to west.

A wooden archway rises to a lofty height of nine metres inside the front gate; it is inscribed with the title which dates back to the reign of the Qing-dynasty Emperor Kangxi: "A Mosque Mandated by His Highness the Emperor" . A stone memorial arch in the second courtyard is carved with the message "Heavenly Supervisor Is Here" ; under the arch stand two stone tablets — the "Imperial-Mandated Stele Marking the Reconstruction of the Mosque" erected during the Wanli Reign of the Ming Dynasty, and the "Stele of the Mosque Granted by the Emperor" erected during the Qianlong Reign of the Qing Dynasty. Both tablets are cut in intaglio, one in the handwriting of the Song-dynasty calligrapher Mi Fu and the other in the handwriting of the Ming-dynasty calligrapher Dong Qichang. Two more stelae are found on both sides of the path leading to the Imperial-Mandated Hall in the third courtyard. One is the "Stele in Memory of Animitta of the Chang'an Mosque" of the Ming Dynasty; the other is the "Moon Stele" inscribed with a text on Islamic astrology written in Arabic by the abbot during the Yongzheng Reign of the Qing Dynasty. The Shengxin Chamber is the highest building in the entire compound. A two-storeyed structure under a three-layered roof with a pointed sloping octagonal roof designed to draw aahing and oohing from the worshipers. In the fourth courtyard stands the Yizhen Pavilion, or Phoenix Pavilion, in the shape of a phoenix on its wings. Set in the tranquility of the courtyard are also a line of wing-rooms laid out with picturesque taste. The Great Summons Hall, large enough to hold a thousand prayers, consists of a frontal veranda, a prayer hall and a rear chamber. All the buildings are elaborated graced with colourful patterns typical of Chinese Islamic structures. The Great Muslim Mosque stands as a unique example in Chinese architecture.

With its tremendous religious influence and precious cultural value, the Muslim Mosque at Huajue Lane has become both a famous religious sanctuary and a tourist attraction, frequented by large crowds of Muslims and tourists all year round.

124

124. The Prayer Hall.
125. A wooden archway.
126. The Shenxing Chamber.

125

126

A World of Dusky Glory: The National Treasures

In ancient times Xi'an was an extensive and well-illuminated showcase of China's resplendent civilization. In return for this great city's generous contributions to the nation's survival, progress and development, history lavished upon it a rich cultural heritage and an all-encapsulating trove of priceless treasures which is the pride of everyone in this country. As part of the world's heritage, this treasurehouse has also provided people throughout the world with much food for thought about the course of society and civilization and about man's inexhaustible creativity.

The historical heritage bestowed on Xi'an and Guanzhong Plain is arrayed in an unusual chronological order commensurate with the area's aged history, an order which is the envy of many other famous historic cities in this world. Stone tools of Lantian Man of the Palaeolithic age more than 1.1 million years ago combine with painted earthenware of the matriarchal Banpo Man 6,000 years ago to form a line along which one can trace the course of evolution of Chinese ancestors in the primitive age. The solemn-looking, mystery-enshrouded Shang and Zhou bronze vessels shed precious light on the pampered lives of slave-owning aristocrats who played ritual music on bronze bells while wining and dining from bronze vessels. The mighty force of combat-ready Qin-dynasty terracotta warriors and Han-dynasty bricks and stones carved with portraiture give authentic expression to the war-torn political atmosphere that permeated Chinese feudalism in its early stage. The dazzling assortment of frescos and gold and silverware are fitting epitaphs for China's feudal society at the apex during the Sui and Tang dynasties, while the countless stone tablets, porcelainware, paintings and calligraphic masterpieces stand testimony to civilization's uninterrupted progress in Xi'an even after it was robbed of emperor-mandated opportunities for prosperity and power. All in all, it is no exaggeration to say that, arranged in a chronological order, the rich cultural heritage of Xi'an and its vicinity is enough to form a comprehensive book of uninterrupted Chinese history.

Abundance is not the only merit of Xi'an's cultural legacy. It is all-embracing as well. Incomplete statistics show that there are as many as 600,000 movable cultural relics in the collections of various museums, not to mention the large historical sites at Western-zhou Feng and Hao, Qin-dynasty Xianyang, Han-Tang Chang'an and the numerous state-of-the-art ancient buildings, famous temples and grottoes. These include ceramics, bronzeware, jadeware, gold and silverware, murals, stone sculptures, brick carvings, stele inscriptions, talismans, seals and whatnot. In a sense, the ancient city of Xi'an is a museum in itself, or an art gallery packed with cultural and art treasures.

Museum Collections

There are seventy-odd museums of all kinds in Shaanxi Province, but the largest of them are mostly found in Xi'an and Guanzhong Plain, such as the Shaanxi Provincial History Museum, Banpo Museum, Stele Forest Museum, Museum of Terracotta Warriors, museums at Maoling, Xianyang, Qianling mausoleums, Famenshi Museum and the Tang-Dynasty Art Museum — all are known for their mammoth collections of high-grade exhibits and each has its unique features. Their collections fall into the following major categories.

127

128

127. Lintong County Museum.
128. Xi'an Museum of Tang-Dynasty Art — Adjacent to the Tang-dynasty Qujiang Pond in the east and the celebrated Tang-dynasty Ci'en Monastery in the west in the Qujiang Scenic Zone on the southern outskirts of Xi'an, this museum with a floorspace of 2,930 square metres is housed in a courtyard fashioned in Tang-dynasty style. Built with joint Chinese and Japanese capital, it was opened to the public in May 1988.
129. Shaanxi Provincial History Museum — Situated to the northwest of the Greater Wild-Goose Pagoda on the southern outskirts of Xi'an, it was completed and opened to the public in June 1991. Covering a total floorspace of nearly 60,000 square metres, the museum is an imposing imitation-Tang structure which houses hundreds of thousands of cultural relics and is known for its vast collections of Sang and Zhou bronzeware and terracotta figurines, as well as gold and silverware and murals from Tang tombs. One of the largest modern museums in China, the Shaanxi Provincial History Museum enjoys the reputation of being a "shining pearl of the ancient capital and a treasure trove in China."

129

Ceramics

Painted earthenware of the Yangshao Culture is one of the most splendid branch of primitive Chinese pottery. The stylized shapes and fascinating patterns on pottery basins with human-mask and fish designs, gourd-shaped earthen jars painted with human faces, and other painted earthenware unearthed from the Banpo and Jiangzhai ruins are a crystallization of our ancestors' penetrating observation and succinct summary of pre-history society; and their long history has rent them a lasting artistic appeal. Chinese ceramics during the period from Shang-Zhou to Qin-Han is marked by a burgeoning utilitarian trend, so much so that ceramic building materials gained wide popularity in and around Xi'an. The highest artistic attainment in this field is seen in decorative tile-ends which were crafted in simple, yet refined designs during the Spring and Autumn Period and the Warring States Period. The patterns on these tile-ends are marked for their unpredictably intricate patterns. Whether in cloudy patterns or the shape of kui-dragons, in the image of exotic-looking animals or of strange flowers and plants, each tile-end is touching in a unique way. Some of the tile-ends are decorated with single or multiple pictographs written in well-proportioned strokes in seal or regular script.

Most of the earthen objects so far unearthed are for burial purposes, with terracotta terracotta figurines of the Qin and Han dynasties accounting for the lion's share. The Tang Dynasty was known for its tri-coloured pottery figurines and utensils glazed in bright and multi-hued colour. Because the most prestigious north Chinese kiln, the Yaozhou Kiln, was situated in Shaanxi, most of the glistening and smooth porcelain products discovered in the province are attributed to Yaozhou. The thirteen smoky-coloured porcelains uncovered from the underground palace of the Famen Monastery in 1987, including bowls, plates, dishes and octagonal vases, are priceless national treasures with their dominant blue colour ingeniously highlighted with a touch of green.

130. Painted pottery basin inscribed with fish designs.

131

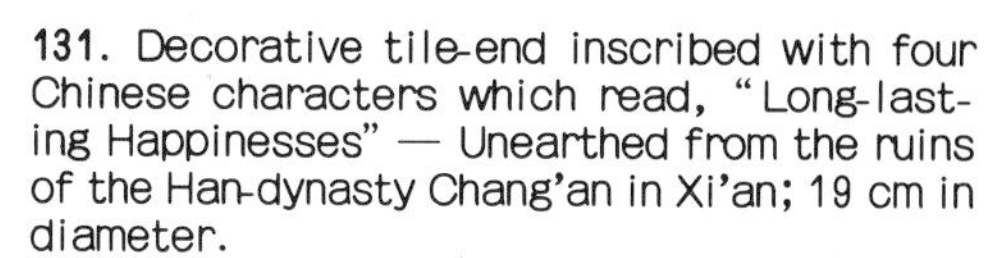

131. Decorative tile-end inscribed with four Chinese characters which read, "Long-lasting Happinesses" — Unearthed from the ruins of the Han-dynasty Chang'an in Xi'an; 19 cm in diameter.

132. Decorative tile-end inscribed with frog patterns — Unearthed from Fengxiang County, Shaanxi Province; about 15 cm in diameter.

133. Decorative tile-end inscribed with four Chinese characters, 17 cm in diameter — Uncovered from the ruins of the Han-dynasty Chang'an on the western outskirts of Xi'an, this decorative tile-end features single-lined tracery with a large knob protruding from its centre. A double-lined cross divides the circles in four fan-shaped sections inscribed with the four Chinese characters in linked smooth brush strokes which mean "The Han Dynasty Reunifies the Country".

132

133

134. Black-glazed bottle in plum-flower designs.

135. Smoky-coloured porcelain bowl — Unearthed from the underground palace of the Tang-dynasty Famen Monastery. About 6.8 cm tall, the statue is covered with an even, smooth and shiny layer of greenish glaze, and it is unusually precious because of the fact that the formula for smoky-coloured glaze was kept a secret for the exclusive use of imperial families in Chinese history. Altogether thirteen such pieces were discovered from the Famen Monastery, which represented a major discovery in Chinese pottery archaeology history.

134

135

136. Blue-and-white porcelain pot in the shape of a figurine.
137. Blue-glazed reverse pot — A 19-cm-tall Song-dynasty piece of art which is ornamented with the vivid image of a lioness breastfeeding her cub. The pot is unique in that its mouth is opened on its bottom, so that it has to be reversed to be filled with water; no leakage is caused when the pot is restored to its usual position.

136

137

139.

◀ 138. Painted terracotta sculpture of a mounted woman wearing a phoenix hat.
139. Terracotta sculpture of a woman in a floor-length robe — Unearthed from the Han-dynasty capital of Xi'an, this figurine stands 31 cm tall, wearing a phoenix hat and a long-sleeved floor-length robe with a wide open bottom. The entire work is marked for its graceful drapery and calm and elegant bearings. It is a rare piece of art among Western-han terracotta figurines.
140. Painted terracotta sculpture of a young woman. ▶

Gold and Silverware

In the earliest days Chinese gold and silverware comprised such tiny ornaments as hooks, buttons as well as odds and pieces designed to beautify daily life. It was not until the Tang Dynasty that the making of gold and silverware really flourished. The discovery of large amounts of gold and silverware from a cellar at Hejiacun Village and the underground palace of the Famen Monastery turned Xi'an and its vicinity into the country's number one sanctum of artifacts in terms of quantity, variety and craftsmanship. The zenith of high-Tang gold and silver smithery is well represented by discoveries made at Hejiacun Village, including a cup made of woven gold filigree, a six-petal silver plate encrusted with bear patterns, a gold-plated silver teapot in the shape of a dancing horse with a cup in its mouth, and walking dragons of pure gold. The highest achievements in this field during the late Tang Dynasty are manifested by a Dharmakaya-carrying bodhisattva, a gold-plated silver incense-burner in the shape of a turtle inscribed with lotus-flower patterns, and a Dharmakaya-welcoming tin staff embellished with silver and gold decorations and twelve rings on two wheels found at the Famen Monastery. The elaborate designs and craftsmanship of the patterns on these gold and silver artifacts are by far unsurpassed by any dynastic age. Rare and priceless gold and silver artifacts have also been unearthed by bits and pieces in various parts of the province. Instances are a gold coffin and silver outer coffin, a gold lotus flower and a gold cane fitted with a silver handle brought to light from the ruins of the Tang-dynasty Qingshan Temple in 1985.

142

141. Tri-coloured pottery of a figurine playing a musical instrument on the back of a camel.

142. Silver outer coffin — Unearthed from the underground palace beneath the Baobeng Temple, Fufeng County, in 1987.

143. Gold and silver tea-set — Unearthed from the underground palace of the Famen Monastery, this is a complete tea-set composed of a tea-miller, a silver cage, and a tortoise-shaped box. Crafted skillfully, this tea-set furnishes important information for the study of tea-related ancient Chinese culture.

143

◀ **144**. Gold teapot carved with flowery patterns, 22.5 cm in diameter — Unearthed from Hejiacun Village in the southern suburb of Xi'an, the pot features a slender neck, a round shoulder and a belly carved with patterns of mandarin ducks, lotus flowers and weed.

145. Gold-plated six-petal silver plate with bear patterns, 13.4 cm in diameter — Unearthed from a Tang-dynasty cellar at Hejiacun Village in the southern suburb of Xi'an, the plate looks unique in that its centre is punched with the gold-plated likeness of a bear.

145

147

146

146. Gold-plated silver plate with double fox patterns, 22.5 cm in diameter — Unearthed from Hejiacun Village in the southern suburb of Xi'an, this silver plate takes the shape of two peaches whose bottoms are each carved with the likeness of a gold-plated fox. The composition is lively with the two foxes looking at each other over the shoulders.

147. Silver tiger, 7 by 11 cm — Unearthed from Shenmu County, Shaanxi Province, the tiger with its hollowed-out round body looks ferocious with a yawning mouth. An ornament for the Xiongnu nomads in the late Warring States Period.

148. Silver Deer.
149. Gold tigers.
150. Seven-layered box — Unearthed from the underground palace of the Tang-dynasty Famen Monastery, this box contained the finger sariars of the Buddha. An enclave within enclaves, the box contains a gold-plated silver box with its lid featuring the likeness of the four Deva-kings, a silk-lidded silver box, a box graced with gold filigree and pearls; and in its heart is placed a stupa-shaped gold container in which the sariars are enshrined.
151. Cup made of woven gold filigree — Unearthed from a Tang-dynasty cellar at Hejiacun Village, Xi'an, this cup measures 5.9 cm in height and 6.8 cm in diameter and weighs 300 grammes. The flowers at the belly and the cloudy patterns at the bottom are made of welded gold filigree; Persian influence is obvious in this cup's decorative style.

148

149

150

151

Bronzeware

Bronzeware is ubiquitous in all the museums in Xi'an and its vicinity. This is because Shaanxi, the cradle of the Zhou people during the Shang dynasty and the seat of the Western-Zhou capitals, is a famed "Land of Bronzeware". Since the Western Han Dynasty history books have recorded a ceaseless stream of discoveries of bronzeware in various phases of historical development. In post-1949 years, the number of bronzeware unearthed with scientific methods have reached as many as 4,000. These include ritual vessels, cooking utensils, wine vessels, food containers, water jars, musical instruments and weapons. There is a complete line of heavy-duty ritual vessels, characterized by bulky sizes and elegant shapes, which belonged to imperial families. About one fourth of the bronzeware so far collected are carved with inscriptions totalling approximately 40,000 characters, or twice as many as the Book of Documents. With topics running the gamut from the use of the vessels and family names to documented ritual and sacrificial events, wars, official appointments and royal endorsements, these inscriptions furnish precious political, military, legal, cultural and economic information for the study of the history of Chinese Bronze Age. The most famous of these heavy-duty bronze vessels are counted by the hundred, such as Shi Qiang's Plate, the Duoyou tripod, the Waishu tripod, a ding with an ogre-mask motif, He zun (wine container), Zhe wine-cup and bronze food containers made to the order of Duke of Li. Shi Qiang's Plate, for example, was cast during the Gongwang Reign of the Western Zhou Dynasty; the 284-character inscription on its bottom has been the longest test among all Western-Zhou bronzeware unearthed since 1949. The text is divided into two parts, the first listing the major achievements of Western Zhou monarchs from King Zhou to King Mu and of the reigning king, the second registering the family history of Shi Qiang, who owned this talisman. Because its inscription offers important data for the study of Shang and Zhou history, this plate is regarded as a milestone in Chinese Bronze Age history. The inside wall of the Duoyou tripod bears a 275-word text which tells of how the royal Zhou family of King Li fought the invading Xianyun nomads (after the Warring States Period they were known as Xiongnu or Huns) from the north and emerged triumphant by driving

152

152. Duke of Qin's Bo — Exhumed from Baoji County, Shaanxi, in 1978 along with two others of the same design but in different sizes, it is a bell-shaped musical instrument of the state of Qin during the Spring and Autumn Period. The bell features four ridges composed of winding bodies of flying dragons and phoenixes. This large bell is cast in a refined taste with rich decorative patterns. A 135-word message is inscribed on it.
153. Shi Qiang's Plate, and a stone rubbing of the inscription on it.

them out of the Zhou territory. The big tripod decorated with ogre-mask designs, which stands 122 cm tall and 83 cm in diameter and weighs 226 kilogrammes, is the largest and heaviest Western-Zhou bronzeware hitherto discovered in China. More bronze masterpieces were produced during the Eastern Zhou, Qin and Han dynasties despite the fact that the Bronze age was drawing to an end and bronze output kept diminishing in those periods. These include Duke of Qin's Bell and Bo (bell with a plane opening and a circular knob on the top) of the Spring and Autumn Period, a gourd-shaped jar with a bird-shaped lid of the Warring States Period, a large painted bronze horse-drawn carriage of the Qin Dynasty, and gold-plated bronze horses, gold-plated silver incense-burners with bamboo-shaped handles, and bronze mirrors of the Han Dynasty. These treasures are in the collections of the Shaanxi Provincial History Museum, the Baoji Municipal Museum and the Zhouyuan Museum.

155

◀ **154.** Gourd-shaped pot with a bird-shaped lid — It is a Warring States Period wine vessel discovered in Suide County. Standing 37.5 cm tall, it takes the shape of a gourd with a bird-like lid, and its belly is inscribed with the bas-relief of six interlaced hydras. The shape is unique, and the ornamental patterns pleasant to the eye.

155. Double-eared square gui vessel — A food container and ritual vessel during the Western Zhou Dynasty, this vessel was unearthed in Boji. At a height of 25 cm, the container features a bell-shaped mouth, curved legs and a square base whose four sides are inscribed with animal-face patterns. The shape is solemn looking and the decorative patterns are vigorous in an elegant way.

156. Duoyou tripod.

157. He zen (wine container) — Discovered from Jiacun Village, Baoji County in 1963, it was a wine container during the reign of King Cheng of the Western Zhou Dynasty. Standing 39 cm tall with a diameter of 28.6 cm, it features a balanced design and well-conceived decorative patterns. King Cheng's 142-word message to his children, inscribed on the bottom of the container, is of important historical reference value.

157

156

158

158. Elephant zun, 23.6 by 37.8 cm — Found at Rujiazhuang Village, Baoji, Shaanxi, in 1974, it is an early Western Zhou wine container in the shape of a robust elephant with an upturned trunk, and the mouth on its back is covered with a double-ringed lid. The vessel is richly decorated with superb flower and phoenix patterns.
159. Great Tripod from Chunhua.
160. Riyi square tripod — Western Zhou wine container, 38.5 cm tall, unearthed in Fufeng County, Shaanxi Province.
161. Painted bronze mirror — Unearthed from the northern outskirts of Xi'an, this bronze mirror is ornamented with curving patterns and painted with vermilion and other colours. It is a priceless treasure, considering the fact that coloured bronze mirror is such a rarity among all Han-dynasty cultural relics.
162. Bronze mirror with patterns of intertwined dragons.

159

160

161

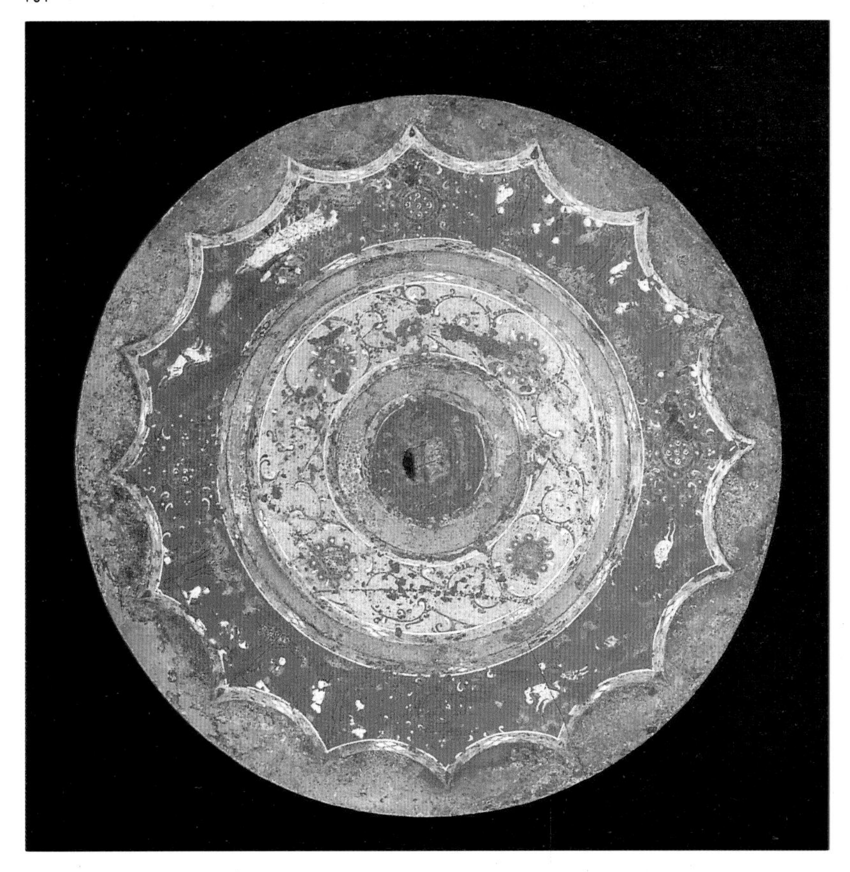

162

Jadeware

The most famous of all the jade carvings unearthed in and around Xi'an are (1) Western-Zhou jadeware uncovered from ruins in Zhouyuan, Baoji, and Feng and Hao in Chang'an, (2) Han-dynasty jadeware from Xianyang, and (3) Tang-dynasty jadeware. The first group consists mainly of ritual and decorative objects in vivid images and patterns such as galloping deer, prancing tigers, docile buffalos and flying birds. The second group features motifs which include bears, eagles, immortal and galloping horse, and most of them are round sculptures skillfully cut out of quality jade. Despite its limited quantity, the third group is marked by superb carving and polishing techniques and, as is shown in a gold-inlaid agate cup in the shape of an animal head, an unmistakable foreign influence.

Apart from these categories, stone sculptures, brick carvings, paintings and calligraphy also occupy a significant position among Xi'an's historical relics. We are obliged to drop mention of them due to the limited space of this book

163

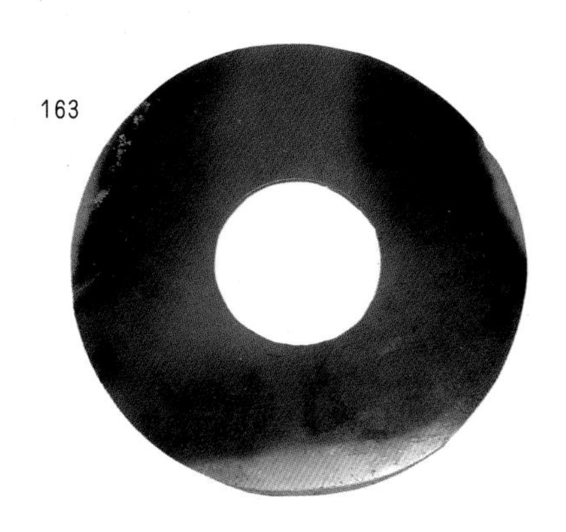

163. Jade carving.

164. Jade immortal and galloping horse, 7 cm in length — Unearthed in Xiangyang, Shaanxi, this object of art was carved during the Western Han Dynasty out of a piece of jade from Hotan, Xinjiang, a place known for its smooth and translucent jade. Both the immortal and the galloping horse look ethereal with wings affixed on their bodies.

165. Agate Cup in the shape of an animal head, 15.6 cm long — Unearthed from a Tang-dynasty cellar at Hejiacun Village on the southern outskirts of Xi'an, this cup is fashioned out of a red piece of agate in a distinct image. With its bright colours it is a rare piece of Tang-dynasty jade carving. ▶

164

165 ▶

166. Jade exorciser, 5.4 by 7 cm, unearthed from Xianyang, Shaanxi.
167. An octagonal jade piece with a round hole in the centre.
168. Jade bear — Another piece of Western Han jade carving 4.8 by 8 cm unearthed from Xianyang, Shaanxi, it features a round-bodied bear walking in a way at once clumsy and lovable.

166

167

168

Frescos in Tang-dynasty Tombs

Frescos, which can be found on the walls of palaces, temples, grottoes and even tombs, are an important part of the Chinese art of painting. Many of them disappeared with the crumbling of the buildings in which they were housed, and so the few that have remained to this day are of unusual value for both collectors and connoisseurs.

Virtually all major master painters of the Tang Dynasty were involved in the making of frescos. As a result, for a time painting on the wall became the mainstream in Chinese painting. Frescos in tombs figured prominently among all the frescos. Tang-dynasty tomb frescos are mostly found in Xi'an and Guanzhong Plain due to the fact that the mausoleums of eighteen Tang monarchs are situated there as well as a huge number of tombs buried with the remains of members of royal families and important officials and generals. Incomplete statistics show that since 1949, frescos ranging in total size from a dozen to several hundred square metres have been found in fifty to sixty Tang-dynasty tombs unearthed in this area. To facilitate research and protection, more than a thousand square metres of them have been stripped from tomb walls. After being consolidated and restored, most of them are now kept in a modern fresco storage of the Shaanxi Provincial History Museum.

The value of Tang-dynasty tomb frescos lies in the fact that their themes came directly from the real life of the deceased's own times. Different from religious frescos and previous works which were mostly of a dedactic nature with the emphasis on extolling ancient sages, most Tang-dynasty frescos are true-to-life pictures of life behind palace walls, hunting scenes, ancient buildings, farming and animal husbandry, exchange with foreign countries, and customs and habits. The Envoys from Friendly Countries from the tomb of Prince Zhanghuai captures a meeting between officials of the Court for Dependencies with convoys from Rome and Mongolia, thereby reflecting in a vivid way the pageantry of diplomatic ceremonies in Chang'an, a city which had fostered extensive contacts with the outside world, and glorifying the monarchy's magnanimous attitudes towards visiting foreigners. Apart from their extensive subject matter, the value of Tang-dynasty tomb frescos also manifests itself in consummate pictorial techniques. Lines are smooth and fluent in a vigorous and often untrammelled fashion; a figure's posture, action, attire, or even personality is brought to vivid life with sparingly executed lines. Coloration is often a ingenious blend of varying hues and colours in perfect harmony or set in striking contrast to yield three-dimensional effects. Thus the settings always look splendid and full of vivacity and figures are often so life-like they seem ready to step out at the viewer's beckoning. Realism is providently combined with well-controlled exaggeration to pump just enough energy and spirits into the men and women that populate the pictures. Palace maids appear more frequently in these frescos than anyone else. Although they are mere servants, yet each and everyone of them is portrayed as a healthy, charming lady who is nobly coiffured, her maidenly face highlighted with rosy cheeks, red lips and curving eyebrows, and has a body that is lithe and pleasing to the eye. Behind the feminine charm one can always sense the presence of an innocent soul.

169

169. A Hunting Procession — This mural, also found in the tomb of Prince Zhanghuai, captures the throng and pageantry of a hunting excursion led by the prince in his life.

171

172

◀ **170**. Painting of a young lady.
171. Envoys from Friendly Countries — This is a mural discovered in the tomb of Prince Zhanghuai of the Tang Dynasty. Of the six figures depicted in the picture, three are court officials and three others are ambassadors in typical foreign imagery and authentic-looking costumes. This picture is important for the study of China's exchanges with foreign countries during the Tang Dynasty.
172. Painting of a young lady.

Calligraphers' Mecca: The Stele Forest

From the viewpoint of a tourist or a historian, the Stele Forest situated on Sanxue Street is enough of a pride for the ancient city of Xi'an and its people. Known variously as a "Massive Pool of Brush and Ink" , "Sanctuary of Calligraphy" and "China's Largest Library on Stones" , this place features a dazzling collection of more than 3, 000 stone tablets which date back as early as the Han Dynasty.

The Xi'an Stele Forest goes back to the late Tang Dynasty and the Five Dynasties. It was first built for the preservation of the Tang-dynasty Book of Filial Piety on Stone Tablets and the Kaicheng Canons on Stones. Acting on a suggestion of Transport Commissioner Lu Dazhong during the Yuanyou Reign of the Northern Song Dynasty, the imperial court moved the canons on stones and other major Tang-dynasty stone tablets to north of the Prefectural Academy, where they formed the basis for the Stele Forest we see today. Since then the Stele Forest has been repeatedly expanded and refurbished. Broken tablets were repaired, and new stone tablets kept arriving. After the founding of the People's Republic, the government, paying due attention to protecting the Stele Forest, conducted large-scale repairs on many occasions. New display pavilions have been added, more trees planted, and researches undertaken for the ways and means to protect the stone tablets from earthquake and other natural adversities. The collection has been constantly replenished with newly discovered tablets and epitaphs of the Han, Jin, Sui and Tang dynasties, and a museum has been established to tighten up management and enhance public awareness. As a result the Stele Forest with its venerated history of nine hundred years has taken on a new life, and its reputation is widespread.

The tremendous historical value of the inscriptions kept in the Stele Forest is best manifested in its major role in preserving and disseminating classical Chinese writings. The Kaicheng Canons on Stones, completed in 838 AD or the second year of the Kaicheng Reign of Emperor Wenzong of the Tang Dynasty, comprises such classics as Book of Changes, Book of Songs, Book of Documents, Rites of Zhou, The Book of Rites, Ceremony and Ritual, Zuo Qiuming's Spring and Autumn Annals, Gongyang's Spring and Autumn Annals, Guliang's Spring and Autumn Annals, Book of Filial Piety, Analects and Er Ya, totalling 650,000 Chinese characters written fastidiously in the regular script. In 754 AD, or the fourth year of the Tianbao Reign, Tang Emperor Xuanzong personally annotated and prefaced the Book of Filial Piety on Stone Tablets, wrote all the texts in the official script, and committed them to stone inscription. Before the invention of the printing technology, these stone inscriptions served as standard textbooks for scholars and students alike. Many of them furnish major historical information about China's friendly and cultural exchanges with foreign countries. Examples in this regard are the "Tablets on the Dissemination of Nestorianism in China during the Qin Dynasty" and the "Stele Dedicated to Monk Amoghavajra" . The former relates how Nestorianism, a sect of Christianity, spread into Chang'an from Central Asia; the later tells the story about a monk from West Territory who disseminated esoteric Buddhism and translated tantric scriptures at Chang'an's Great Xingshan Temple, and whose disciple Huiguo (807-883 AD) indoctrinated the Japanese monk Kukai (774-835 AD) with tantric principles, enabling esoteric Buddhism to spread to Japan. These historical records are of invaluable reference value for the study of the history of exchanges between China and foreign countries and the origin and development of religion in China. Major historical data can also be derived from large numbers of Tang-dynasty epitaphs and Ming and Qing-dy-

173. A rubbing from the stele in commemoration of Cao Quan.
174. A rubbing of part of the stone tablet inscribed with a prescription for the treatment of stomachache.
175. A rubbing of a stone tablet in the Yan Family Temple.
176. A display gallery in the Stele Forest.

173

174

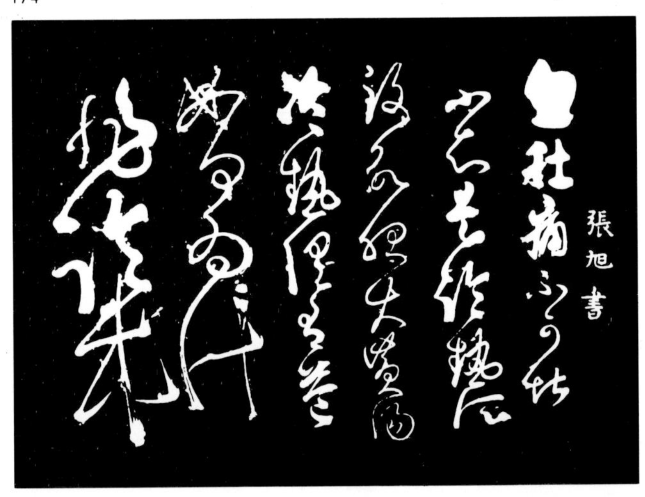

大達法師玄秘塔碑銘
夫兼御史中丞上柱國
兼判院事上柱國賜紫
仁義禮樂輔
尚其出家之雄乎天水
大弘法教言訖而滅既
歲依崇福寺道悟禪師

175

nasty stone inscriptions preserved in the Stele Forest. The historical information contained in this mammoth library-on-stone will, with the progress of scholarly researches, draw increasing attention from all walks of life.

Added to the Stele Forest's historic value is its universally recognized high artistic attainments. Here, calligraphy as a unique Chinese art is comprehensively represented in an ocean of stone inscriptions, which encompasses virtually all celebrated Chinese calligraphers through the ages, whose masterpieces are available in all four major scripts — seal, official, regular and cursive. In the seal script, the Song-dynasty "Yishan Stone Inscription" in the well-disciplined handwriting of Li Si of the Qin Dynasty features the earliest standard script after the unification of the Chinese written form. Another superb work in Qin-dynasty seal script is found in the "Epitaph to Three Graves" written by Li Yangbing, a Tang-dynasty calligrapher. In the official or clerical script, representative works include the "Stele of Cang Jie's Temple", "Stele for the House of the Immortal Tang" and "Stone Tablet in Memory of Cao Quan" of the Han Dynasty, as well as the "Stone Tablet in Memory of a Zen Master of Great Wisdom", "A Message to the Sacred Mount Huashan" and Book of Filial Piety on Stone Tablets of the Tang Dynasty, but the "Stone Tablet in Memory of Cao Quan" wrought in 185 AD or the second year of the Zhongping Reign of the Eastern Han Dynasty is the most famous of them all. Carved on a darkish, shiny stone slab of superb quality in a style which is meticulous in an elegant and natural way, the inscription has been a favorite with epigraphers and calligraphers through the generations as a finest example of the official script during its heyday in the

176

◀ 177. A stone tablet in the Yan Family Temple.

178. Statue of a female bodhisattva — With head and limbs missing, the statue stands 90 cm tall. Her bosomy, slender body which is bejewelled and partially clad with a thin layer of gauze exudes the charm of a mature woman. For this it is regarded as Venus of the East.

178

Eastern Han Dynasty. In the cursive or "grass" script, "A Composition of a Thousand Words" written by Tang-dynasty Zhang Xu and Huai Su, jokingly nicknamed "Eccentric Zhang and Crazy Su", is astonishing for its brush strokes that by turns skitter, swirl, soar and plunge in an utterly freewheeling manner. As a matter of fact, Zhang Xu's calligraphic works are known as one of the "three wonders" of the Tang Dynasty along with Li Bai's poems and Fei Min's sword playing. Huai Su, who inherited Zhang Xu's art in an innovative way, came up with a style of his own; Li Bai the Tang poet went so far as to extol Zhang's cursive style as "unparalleled under heaven". The Stele Forest has no lack of outstanding works in the semi-cursive and regular scripts as well. The "Poem on a Travel to Tianguan Mountain" in the handwriting of Zhao Mengfu, a well-known Yuan-dynasty calligrapher and painter, is executed in bravura brushwork made possible with smooth and vehement strokes. The "Preface to the Sacred Teachings of Tripitaka of the Great Tang" was carved by Monk Huairen during the Xianheng Reign of the Tang Dynasty by knocking together characters written by the great Jin-dynasty calligrapher Wang Xizi; though an assembled work, it does justice to Wang's lyrical and fluid art in a highly integral composition. Visitors to the Stele Forest also have the opportunity to see works by three of the four major Song-dynasty calligraphers Me Fu, Su Shi and Huang Tingjian. Fine examples in the regular script include Ouyang Xun's "Epitaph to Huangpu Yan", Lu Shinan's "Stele for the Hall of the Confucian Temple", Zhu Suiliang's "Preface-on-Stele to the Holy Teachings of Tripitaka in Tongzhou", Yan Zhenqing's "Tablet on a Spiritual Response to the Multi-Treasure Pagoda", "Stone Tablet in Tribute to Yan Qin" and "Stele for the Temple of the Yans", and Liu Gongquan's "Stone Tablet for the Xuanmi Pagoda" — all these men were gurus in Chinese calligraphy history, and their works are still being emulated and extolled today.

Apart from these calligraphic epitaphs, the Stele Forest Museum of Xi'an also operates a gallery which displays an impressive line of stone carvings, most of them being tomb stone carvings and religious statues which reflect the social mores and artistic aspirations of people during the Han, Wei Jin, Sui Tang, Song and Ming dynasties.

A Modern Metropolis Forges Ahead

Xi'an, an ancient capital steeped in the glory of a venerable three-millennia history, is moving ahead sure-footed towards a bright future.

The birth of the People's Republic in 1949 opened a new chapter in the city's annals. Riding the high tide of reform and opening to the outside world since the 1980s, the 6.5 million Xi'an people have made breakthroughs in all fields of endeavour — science and technology, tourism, commerce, foreign trade, etc. — and are making concerted effort to turn their city into a socialist metropolis with a global outlook.

Xi'an as it is today has become an important centre for China's scientific and technological research and development. There are more than three thousand research institutes in machine-building, power, electronics, aviation, aeronautics, geology, chemical, textile, instrument and apparatus, and nuclear industries. Every year researchers in Xi'an come up with a rich crop of major scientific results, many of which reach or approach advanced international levels. The newly established Xi'an High and New Technology Development Zone has pumped new vigor and life into local economy by transferring research results into productivity. As far as comprehensive scientific and technical strength goes, Xi'an ranks third among the nation's large cities, second only to Beijing and Shanghai.

Xi'an is a major centre for higher learning. Scattered all over the city are forty-two universities and colleges and a dozen or so mobile post-doctorate research centres. A hundred or so departments are eligible to confer doctorate degrees and more than three hundred of them offer courses which lead to a master's degree. Xi'an is indeed a cradle for high-calibre professionals.

Xian has also become a world-famous tourist centre. With its ocean of historical and cultural legacies, majestic and picturesque landscape typical of the Northwest, and imbued with exotic folklore in unparalleled diversity, Xi'an is an irresistible temptation for holiday-makers and sightseers around the world.

Xi'an of today is a landlocked international metropolis. The city has established extensive ties with more than a hundred countries and regions; it has fostered sister relationships with twelve cities, such as Kyoto, Nara and Funabashi of Japan, Kansas City of the United States, Lahore of Pakistan, Isfahan of Iran, Pau of France, Edinburg of the United Kingdoms, Dortmus of Germany, Kyongju of South Korea, Dnipropetrovsk of Ukraine, and Iasi of Romania. Such burgeoning relations with various parts of the world are evocative of the pomp and pageant of the Tang-dynasty Chang'an, where the streets were thronged with foreigners in all manners of exotic attire and merchants hawked their wares in a hundred and one different dialects; the only difference between today and yesterday is that the relations of present-day Xi'an with other parts of the world have acquired a more profound and sophisticated cultural meaning.

History has treated Xi'an ever so kindly. Xi'an, in return, will never let history down.

179. An ancient cultural street at Shuyuan-men.
180. South Avenue, Xi'an.

179

180

181

181. Satellite Monitoring Centre at Xi'an.
182. The Xi'an High and New Technology Development Zone under construction.
183. Night scene in the city's commercial area.
184. Second Southern Ring Road.
185. The Xi'an-Lintong Expressway.

182

183

184

185

186

187

188

189

186. Xincheng Plaza, Xi'an.
187. Giant panda, an endangered species.
188. A glimpse of the campus of the Xi'an Jiaotong University.
189. The Xi'an Botanical Garden.

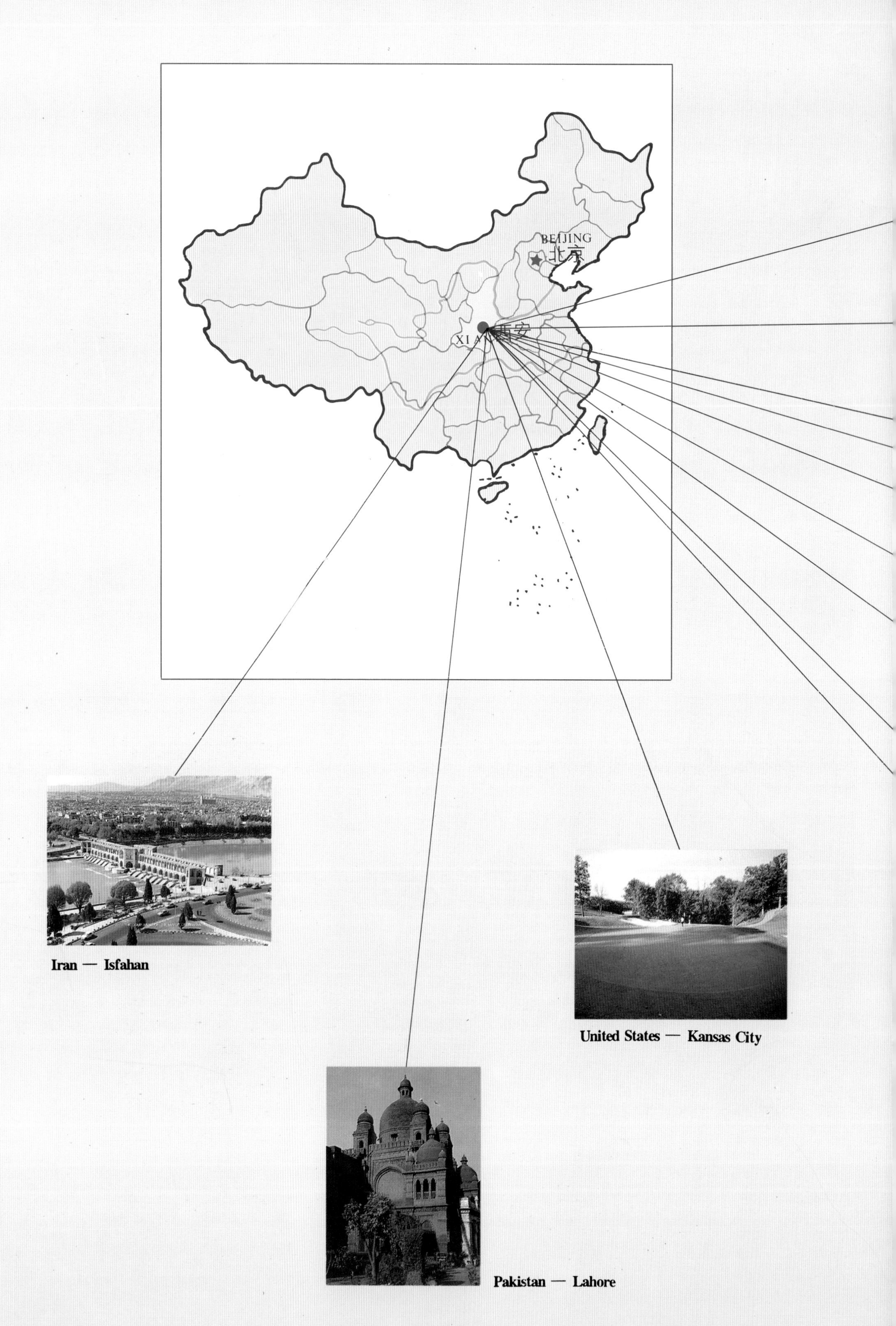

Iran — Isfahan

United States — Kansas City

Pakistan — Lahore

A Map of Cities which Have Sister Relations with Xi'an

Republic of Korea — Kyongju

France — Pau

Ukraine — Dnipropetrovsk

Japan — Nara

Japan — Kyoto

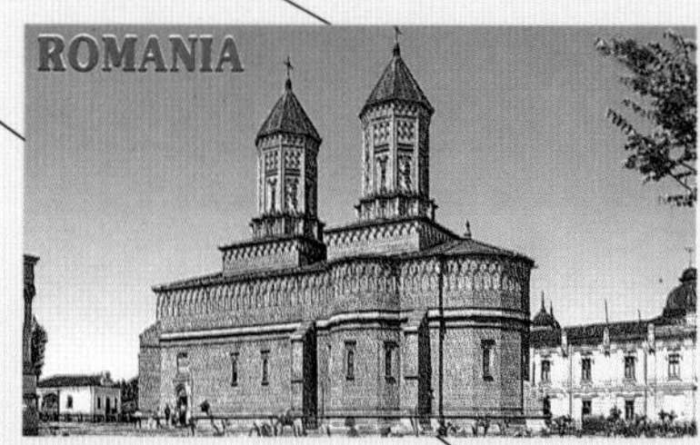

Romania — Iasi

Germany — Dortmus

Japan — Funabashi

United Kingdoms — Edinburg

Major Historical Events in Xi'an and Vicinity

Bronze tripod with interlocked cloudy patterns.

Beacon Tower on the Lishan Mountain.

King Wu of Zhou Eliminates Shang and Establishes His Capital at Hao — During the llth century BC, the Zhou people gradually emerged on the political scene, and King Wen of Zhou moved his capital from Zhouyuan at the foot of the Qishan Mountain to Feng by the Feng River west of present-day Xi'an. After his death his son took the throne as King Wu, who expanded the old capital and built the new capital Hao opposite Feng across the river. At the time, contradictions in the Shang court were intensified by King Zhou's debauchery and tyranny, and "the populace were greatly discontented, and duke after duke began to betray him", as a history book puts it. Taking advantage of this opportunity, King Wu of Zhou pledged alliances with various dukes and declared war on King Zhou. During the Battle of Muye, Shang-dynasty generals and soldiers rose in rebellion one after another. At his wit's end King Zhou burned himself to death. In 1027 BC, a triumphant King Wu returned to Hao, where he established the Zhou Dynasty. Historians refer to his regime as Western Zhou Dynasty.

Bonfire at Lishan Plays a Trick on Dukes; with a Mere Smile the Beauty Spoils the King's Rule — Towards the end of the Western Zhou Dynasty, King You abandoned himself to debauchery and sensual pleasure with his favorite concubine Bao Si, to the neglect of government affairs. At the time the Zhou was busy fighting the western Rongdi nomads, and a beacon tower was erected atop the Lishan Mountain in present-day Lintong County to facilitate communication with the forefront. One day, just to make Bao Si happy, the king had a bonfire raised on the tower. Dukes rushed to his rescue from all over the country, only to return in great exasperation. In 771 BC, Duke of Shen mounted a large-scale attack on the Zhou capital city of Hao in league with the Quanrong nomads. King You signalled an SOS by making a bonfire atop the Lishan Mountain, but not a single soldier came to his rescue. As a result the Quanrong soldiers stormed into Hao without so much as a decent fight. While fleeing for his life King You was killed at the foot of Lishan. The Western Zhou Dynasty came to an ignominious end.

Decorative tile-end with cloudy patterns.

A Qin-dynasty dagger axe.

Shang Yang's Reform — In the early years of the Warring States Period, the state of Qin was nothing but a weakling among the dukedoms. After Duke Xiao of Qin took the throne, he keenly felt that "it is a great shame for Qin to be looked down upon by the dukes". So he scouted for someone who could help him reform the system. In 359 BC, he appointed Shang Yang militia general and authorized him to introduce reform measures, which included dividing households into groups of five or ten which were responsible for one another's behaviour, rewarding those who reported on criminal acts, honouring those who distinguished themself on the battlefield while forbidding private fights, boosting farming and curtailing commerce, rewarding those engaged in ploughing and weaving, abolishing the patriarchal clan system, and introducing a system for the grading of military merits. Nine years later Shang Yang carried out the second round of his reform, establishing an administrative system at county, township and village levels, promoting a new land distribution system, and unifying the weights and measures. Thanks to these measures, the state of Qin rose quickly as a powerful state and accomplished the transition from slave society to feudalism. Shang Yang's reform thus came down in history as a milestone in the social progress of ancient China.

State of Qin Conquers Six Rival States and Unifies the Country — In 230 BC, King Ying Zheng of Qin kicked off the war to unify the country with an army of several hundred thousand soldiers. After a decade of bloody war, he eliminated the six rival states of Han, Zhao, Yan, Wei Chu and Qi, thereby putting an end to centuries of national estrangement in the hands of warring dukes. In 221 BC, he established the Qin Dynasty, the first centralized feudal empire in Chinese history. To consolidate his rule he ordered that the written language, law, the gauge and weights and measures be standardized. He also abolished the enfeoffment system and instituted a prefecture-county system. These measures helped promote feudal economic and cultural development and laid down the political principles which were to prolong Chinese feudalism for the next two thousand and more years.

The valley where Confucian scholars were buried alive under the rule of Qinshihuang.

Hongmen, a fortification in Lintong County.

Qinshihuang Burns Books and Buries Confucian Scholars Alive — To fortify his autocracy after unifying China, the founding emperor of the Qin Dynasty, Qinshihuang, pursued high-handed policies in ideological and cultural fields. In 213 BC, acting on Prime Minister Li Si's opinion that Confucian scholars were jeopardizing the rule of the monarch by using books to "extol the past and negate the present", Qinshihuang ordered that with the exception of those written by Qin historians all history books and works by scholars of different schools of thought be handed in and burned, thereby committing unprecedented vandalism with classical Chinese culture. A year later, having failed in his search for the pill of immortality, he vented his spleen by having several hundred Confucian scholars buried alive in Xianyang and Lintong on charges of rumour-mongering and slanders. This cruel action incurred national fury and speeded up the downfall of the Qin Dynasty.

Banquet at Hongmen Contrived as a Trap — As the Qin Dynasty floundered on its last legs, it was confronted with large-scale attacks by uprising armies led by Liu Bang and Xiang Yu respectively. Despite his inferior force, Liu Bang upstaged Xiang Yu and conquered Xianyang. Greatly enraged, in 206 BC Xiang Yu directed his 400,000-strong army to Xixi (east of present-day Lintong) in a showdown with Liu Bang, whose 100,000 troops were stationed at Bashang. Having unwittingly divulged his secret, Liu Bang personally went to Hongmen to apologize to Xiang Yu, thus setting the scene for what is historically known as the Hongmen Banquet. During the feast, Fan Zhen, an advisor, hinted repeatedly for Xiang Yu to assassinate his opponent. But Xiang Yu did not oblige. Then the advisor invited Xiang Yu to play the sword by the table so that he could take the opportunity and kill Liu Bang. Due partly to Xiang Bo's protection and partly to Xiang Yu's hesitation, Liu Bang was able to flee the banquet unscathed. The Chu-Han scramble for supremacy ended with the defeat of Xiang Yu, who committed suicide by slitting his own throat. Liu Bang, emerging triumphant, established the Western Han Dynasty.

A camel caravan on the Silk Road.

Tomb of Huo Qubing.

Zhang Qian, on a Diplomatic Mission to West Territory, Opens up the Silk Road —yuezhi kingdom so that a pincer attack could be launched to conquer the Xiongnu nomads, sent Zhang Qian on a mission to the West Territory. In 138 BC, Zhang Qian and his entourage of a hundred set off from Xi'an. He returned to Chang'an thirteen years later, having undergone untold hardships and passed what are today's Fergana, Samarkand and north of the Armu River. His was the first government delegation ever sent to the West in Chinese history. In 119 BC, Zhang Qian was dispatched as the Han emissary for a second time to the West Territory. Both missions helped disseminate Chinese silks, porcelainware, iron implements and farming techniques to central Asian countries and enabled the Chinese to learn something about the culture, geography, resources, habits and customs in these countries. The long and winding Euroasian footpath opened by Zhang Qian has since been known as the Silk Road.

Huo Qubing Has It Out with the Xiongnu — Huo Qubing (140-117 BC), a celebrated general during the Western Han Dynasty, rose to the rank of Cavalry General-in-Chief in return for his brilliant military service. After his death he was decorated as "Duke and Commander-in-Chief". During the reign of Emperor Wu, the northern Xiongnu nomads made repeated inroads into the Han territory, killing and looting the local people along the way. Following the emperor's order in 121 BC, or the second year of the Yuanshou Reign, General Huo beat the Xiongnu on two occasions, took control of the entire area west of the Yellow River and opened the Silk Road to traffic once again. In 119 AD, or the fourth year of the Yuanshou Reign, he and another general, Wei Qing, drive straight into enemy turf and defeated the Xiongnu's main force. When Emperor Wu offered to build him a luxury mansion, he turned it down, saying, "When the Xiongnu are still around, how can I make my home?" In his life he had launched six expeditions on the Xiongnu and performed meritorious service in safeguarding peace and territorial integrity of the Han Dynasty.

Temple of Sima Qian.

Swallowing the Insult, Sima Qian Writes "Records of the Historian" — Sima Qian, a native of Xiayang (present-day Hancheng, Shaanxi Province) who began writing the Records of the Historian during his tenure as Grand Astrologer during the reign of Emperor Wu of the Western Han Dynasty. Because he had spoken in defence of Prime Minister Li Ling, he was incriminated and punished by castration. Swallowing this major humiliation, he threw himself into his book. In 93 AD, after nearly two decades of hard work, he eventually completed the magnum opus Records of the Historian. As China's first general history book written in an chronological order which covers three thousand years of Chinese history from the legendary Yellow Emperor to Emperor Wu of the Western Han Dynasty, the book amounts to 520,000 words in 130 chapters and is extolled for its all-inclusive contents, penetrating exposition and lucid and elegant writing style.

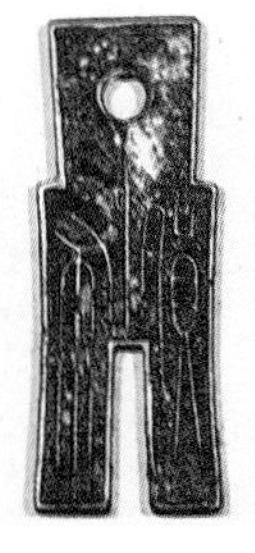

Currency of the Xinmang Reign.

Wang Mang Usurps the Throne — Wang Mang (45 BC-23 AD), whose style name was Jujun, was a nephew of the wife of Emperor Yuan of the Han Dynasty. During the reign of Emperor Pingdi, Wang served as Chancellor of Military Affairs. In that capacity he knocked together a clique of henchmen and elbowed dissidents out of his way. In 5 AD or the fifth year of the Yuanshi Reign, Wang Mang poisoned Emperor Pingdi to death, and, by delivering a false imperial edict, made himself the emperor under the new reign title "Xin". He put all the land in the nation under the family name "Wang" and banned slave trades. To increase the country's tax revenue, he wreaked financial havoc by overhauling the monetary system repeatedly. In 17 AD or the fourth year of the Tianfeng Reign, nationwide peasant uprisings broke out, and the forces of the imperial Han family overran Chang'an. In the melee Wang Mang was killed and his short-lived regime came to an end. Two years later, Liu Xiu founded the Eastern Han Dynasty.

Landscape north of the Great Wall.

Wang Shaojun Married North to Xiongnu — The northern Xiongnu nomads had been a menace to the political power of Central China since the Zhou and Qin dynasties. By the early Western Han Dynasty, the Xiongnu became so powerful that they made repeated incursions southward, burning, killing and looting all at once along the way. The Western Han Dynasty was forced to pacify the Xiongnu rulers by marrying daughters of the imperial family to them. In 33 BC, Wang Qiang, a servant maid whose literary name was Shaojun, volunteered to be married to Huhanye, a Xiongnu chieftain. During her decades' stay at the Xiongnu territory as Chieftain's Consort, she made tremendous contributions to fraternity between the Hans and the Xiongnu nomads. Her deeds have inspired men of letters of later generations, who have written large numbers of poems and opera scripts in eulogy of her.

Stone rhinoceros at the Xianling Mausoleum.

Li Yuan Becomes the Father of the Tang Dynasty — In its twilight years the Sui Dynasty was shaken to the core by wave upon wave of peasant uprisings. Li Yuan, rear commander of Taiyuan, rose in arms against the Sui monarch and launched a pincer attack with his eldest son Li Jiancheng serving as commander of the left flank and his second son Li Shimen as commander of the right flank. With the coordination of other resurgent armies, he quickly fought his way into Chang'an. He first installed Yan You, grandson of the Sui Emperor Yang, as the puppet emperor and made himself prime minister. In 618 AD, when news came that Emperor Yang had been killed in Jiangdu, Li Yuan ascended the throne and became the founding emperor of the Tang Dynasty with Chang'an as the capital.

Portrait of Li Shimin, who founded the Tang Dynasty.

Coup D'etat at Xuanwu Gate — After he established the Tang Dynasty, Li Yuan made his eldest son Li Jiancheng the Crown Prince and his second son Li Shimin Prince of Qin. Jealous of the high reputation his younger brother had earned for his meritorious service in unifying the country and establishing the new empire, the crown prince conspired against Li Shimin's life in league with the emperor's fourth son Li Yuan, or Prince of Qi. In 626 AD, Li Shimin and the generals of his Qin Mansion laid an ambush inside the Xuanwu Gate north of the Hall of Supreme Being. When Li Jianmin and Li Yuan appeared on the scene, they rushed out on horseback and killed the two princes. This incident is known in Chinese history as "Coup D'etat at Xuanwu Gate" . Li Yuan, now Emperor Gaozu, had no choice but to install Li Shimin as Crown Prince. Shortly afterwards, he voluntarily abdicated and assumed the title "Super Sovereign" . Li Shimin succeeded the throne and became Emperor Taizong.

The Sun-and-Moon Mountain in Qinh

Princess Wencheng in Tibet — A member of the family of Emperor Taizong, or Li Shimin, Princess Wencheng was married to the king of Tubo Songtsan Gambo in 641 AD or the twenty-fifth year of the Zhenguan Reign of the Tang Dynasty, having journeyed with a large entourage across the vast wilderness of the Qinghai-Tibet Plateau and bringing to Tibet a heavy load of Buddhist scriptures, canonical writings, vegetable seeds, silkworm eggs and drugs. After her arrival the princess taught the local people how to plough the land, raise cocoons and weave cloth, make earthenware, use the calendar, make paper and brew wine. She also helped Songtsan Gambo create the written Tibetan language, thereby giving a great impetus to the political, economic and cultural development of her adopted land. Stories in eulogy of her great contributions are still current among the Tibetan people.

Xuan Zang's Pilgrimage to the West — In 629 AD, Xuan Zang, a celebrated Chinese monk, embarked on a solitary western-bound journey along the Silk Road. Four years later, having experienced untold hardships, sometimes narrowly escaping with his life, he arrived in India, where he apprenticed himself to Buddhist gurus, read extensively and eventually emerged as a top-notch Buddhist scholar. In 645 AD, he returned to Chang'an, settled down at the Ci'en Monastery, and began translating the six hundred and more scriptures he had brought back with him. In the intervening years he translated 74 scriptures in 1,335 volumes, a feat which is without parallel in translation history.

The celebrated monk Xuan Zang with his load of books.

Stone horses at Qianling Mausoleum.

Wu Zetian, China's First Female Monarch — Wu Zetian used to be a favorite concubine of Emperor Taizong who renamed her "Wu Mei" , meaning "Charming Lady Wu" . After the death of the emperor she was tonsured and became a nun in the Ganye Nunnery. The new emperor, Gaozong, reinstalled her in the imperial palace and made her Lady Shaoyi. In 655 AD, he deposed his empress in favour of Wu Zetian. As the emperor's health declined steadily, the new empress was able to show her talent in handling the country's political affairs. After the emperor died, she deposed the two succeeding emperors, Zhongzong and Ruizong; in 690 AD, breaking the rule that banned an empress from ascending the throne, she made herself the "Holy Emperor" , changed the name of the dynasty to Zhou, and became the only female monarch in Chinese history.

Stone horses at Qianling Mausoleum.

The Celebrated Poet Li Bai Enters Chang'an — Li Bai, the great Tang-dynasty romantic poet who cherished the ambition to "save the multitude and bring peace to the country" since childhood, is deified as "God of Poetry" in this country. In 730 AD, Li Bai visited Chang'an for the first time in his life, but, his talent unappreciated, he left the capital city in great disappointment. In 742 AD, an imperial edict summoned him back to Chang'an, where he was treated royally and composed a great number of poems. The ensuing three years marked the apogee of his literary career. Li Bai abhorred bowing and scraping to those in high power. Legend has it that during one poem-composing session with the emperor, he had the monarch's chief eunuch Gao Lieshi take off his shoes and Lady Yang hold the inkslab for him. This story about Li Bai's self-pride and untrammelled personality has been told and retold among the Chinese through the ages.

Tomb of Imperial Lady Yang.

Mutiny at Mawei — After the An Lushan-Shi Siming Rebellion broke out in 756 AD or the fifteenth year of the Tianbao Reign, Emperor Xuanzong and his favorite concubine Lady Yang were forced to flee for life under the protection of a number of trusted ministers and generals and several hundred imperial guards. When the procession stopped over at the Mawei Courier Station in present-day Xingping County, Shaanxi Province, the imperial guards rose in mutiny, killing the treacherous minister Yang Guozhong and forcing the emperor to have Lady Yang commit suicide by hanging herself in the prayer hall of the courier station. Stopping at Mawei on his way home from Sichuan after the An-Shi Rebellion had been quelled, Emperor Xuanzong issued a secret instruction to have the body of his favorite concubine buried by the wall of the station. Today the tomb is still there, along with a marble statue of the beautiful woman.

A monument to Abeno Nakamaro.

Japan Dispatches Emissaries to Tang — China and Japan are neighbours separated by a mere strip of the Pacific. During the Tang Dynasty, friendly exchanges took place frequently between the two countries. Japan had dispatched group after group of students and monks to study in Chang'an. During the 260-odd years from Emperor Taizong to Emperor Shaozong, Chang'an received nineteen Japanese delegations, with the number of a single delegation reaching as high as 650. During their stay in the capital city, the Japanese were received by the emperor repeatedly. Nakamaro, a Japanese student, stayed in Chang'an for fifty-four years until his death. After they had finished their studies, Ennin (793-864 AD) and Kukai (774835 AD) returned to Japan bringing with them large numbers of Tang books, and made major contributions to the development of Sino-Japanese friendship.

Ruins of the Daming Palace.

The city of Xi'an during the Ming Dynasty.

Zhu Wen Topples the Tang Dynasty — Towards the end of the Tang Dynasty, the peasant uprising led by Huang Chao broke out. A speculator named Zhu Wen joined the ranks and fought his way into Chang'an, where he was promoted to the position of Great General. Before long he surrendered himself to the Tang court and worked in league with other warlords in suppressing the Huang Chao peasant uprisers. For his contributions Emperor Xizong changed his name to Zhu Quanzhong (Zhu the Loyal Man). As a result, his military strength grew steadily. When the newly enthroned Emperor Shaozong had been kidnapped by a number of eunuchs and Li Maozhen who was military governor of Fengxiang, Prime Minister Cui Yin turned to Zhu Wen for help. Zhu responded by dispatching his army in a rout of Li Maozhen, killing the eunuchs and seizing the emperor back. He then forced the emperor to move the capital to Luoyang, evacuated the residents and razed Chang'an to the ground. In 904 AD, Zhu Wen killed Emperor Zhaozong, and installed Emperor Aidi on the throne. In 907 AD, he deposed and killed the new emperor, made himself the emperor and changed the dynasty name to Liang, with Kaifeng as the capital. Historians call his regime the Late Liang Dynasty, which spelled the end of the great Tang empire. And the position of Chang'an as the nation's capital was no more.

Li Zicheng Establishes the Dashun Regime — As the Ming Dynasty tottered on its last legs, the situation was aggravated by massive famine which broke out in Shaanxi. Li Zicheng, a Shaanxi native, took part in a peasant uprising and in a matter of years, his force fought its way across Shaanxi, Shanxi, Henan, Hubei, Anhui, Sichuan, Gansu and other provinces, and grew to a million troops. In 1643, Li Zicheng conquered Tongguan, and on November 11 of the same year, his troops entered Xi'an, the most important city in northwest China. In 1644, Li Zicheng proclaimed the establishment of the Yongchang reign of his new regime, the Dashun Dynasty, which became yet another peasant regime in Xi'an following Liu Bang and the Chimei Uprising during the Han Dynasty and Huang Chao during the Tang Dynasty.

The Revolutionary Park, Xi'an.

The Pavilion in memory of the Xi'an Incident.

Defending Xi'an under the Command of "Twin Tigers" — In 1926, with the support of warlords Wu Peifu and Yan Xishan, the 100,000-strong force under Liu Zhenhua, a Henan reactionary warlord, mounted an attack on Xi'an. The city was guarded by the National Army with a little more than 10,000 men under the command of Li Huchen (commander of the Second Army) and Yang Hucheng (who commanded the Third Division of the Third Army). The siege lasted several months, and more than 50,000 died of hunger or cold in the city, but under the leadership of the "twin tigers" (each man's name contains the Chinese character "tiger") the civilians and armymen, sharing a burning hatred for the enemy, vowed to live or die with the ancient city. In October, patriotic generals Feng Yuxiang and Yu Youren came to Xi'an's rescue, routing Liu Zhenhua's troops on November 27. The battle to defend Xi'an thus came to a triumphant end. However, the war has left its ugly marks in the hearts of the city's people. The Revolutionary Park situated on Fifth West Road was built to bury the remains of those who fell in defending the city.

The Xi'an Incident — After the September 18th Incident of 1931, the anti-Japanese movement for national salvation surged throughout China. The Nanjing government headed by Chiang Kai-shek, sticking to its anti-communist policy and bent on waging a civil war, ordered the Northeast Army headed by Zhang Xueliang and the Northwest Army commanded by Yang Hucheng to attack the Red Army stationed in Shaanxi. In December 1936, Chiang Kai-shek arrived in Xian. The two generals, out of patriotic enthusiasm and indignation against Chiang's callousness to the nation's destiny, took the resolute step of a military showdown to remonstrate with the leader. On December 12, they arrested Chiang Kai-shek at the Huaqing Palace, Lintong, and published an open telegram to the nation demanding for an end to civil war and unity in fighting the Japanese. Through the mediation of a Communist Party delegation and other organizations, Chiang was released after accepting the condition to "stop the civil war and unite with the Communists in combating the Japanese invaders". The peaceful settlement of the Xi'an Incident turned the tables in favour of anti-Japanese war efforts.

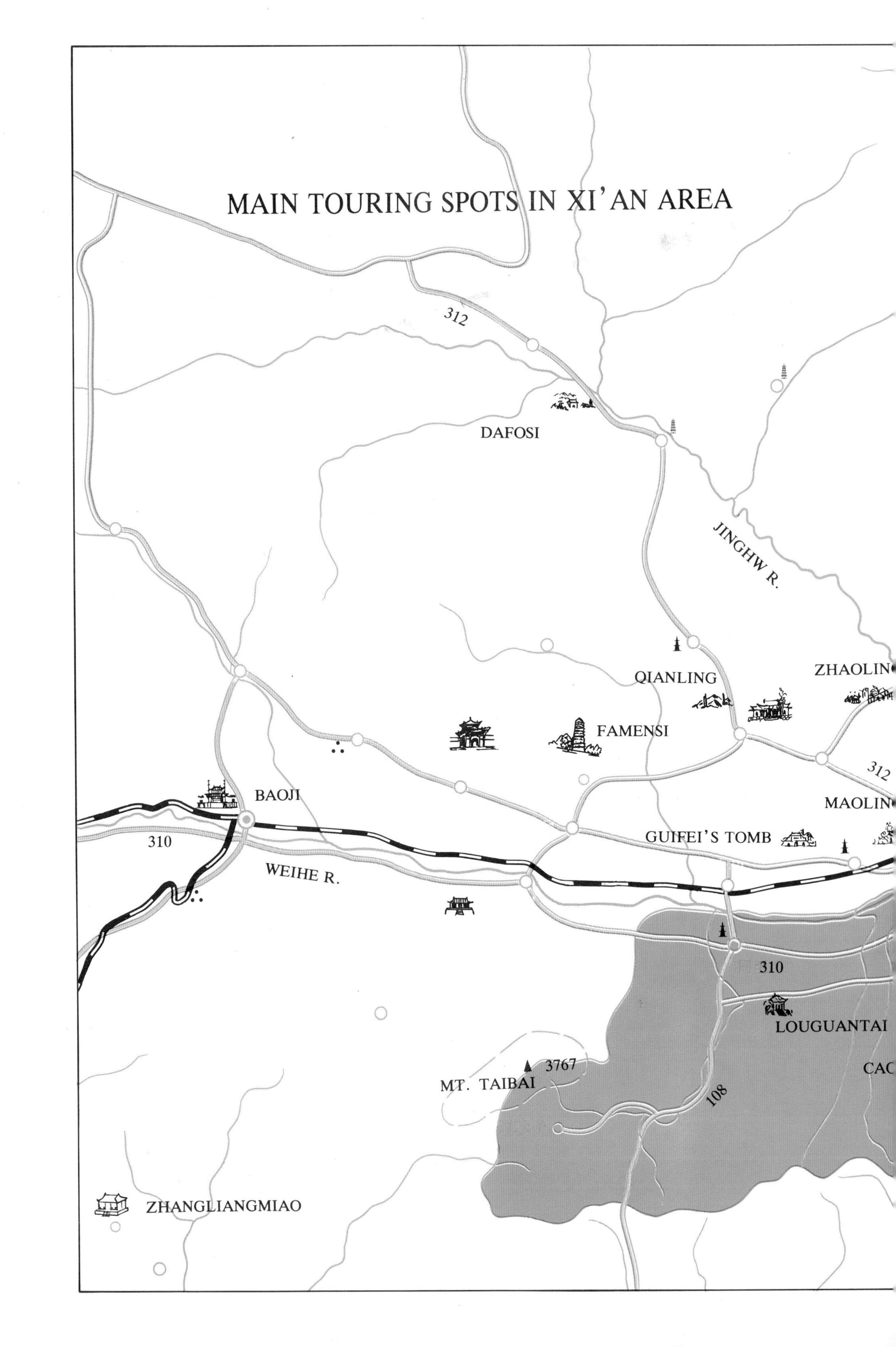

MAIN TOURING SPOTS IN XI'AN AREA
312
DAFOSI
JINGHW R.
QIANLING
ZHAOLIN
FAMENSI
312
BAOJI
MAOLIN
310
GUIFEI'S TOMB
WEIHE R.
310
LOUGUANTAI
3767
MT. TAIBAI
108
ZHANGLIANGMIAO

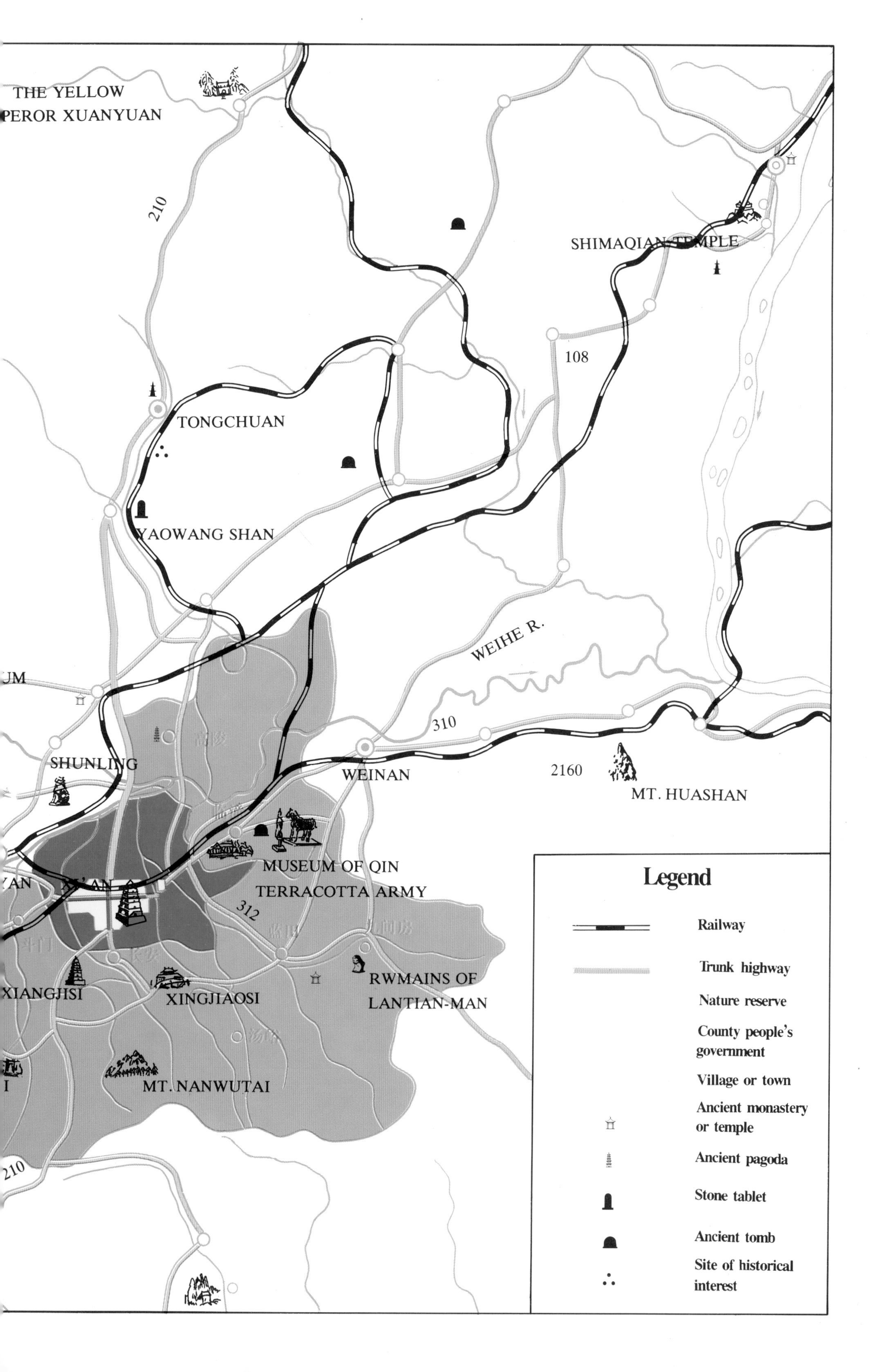
THE YELLOW
PEROR XUANYUAN
210
SHIMAQIAN TEMPLE
108
TONGCHUAN
YAOWANG SHAN
WEIHE R.
UM
SHUNLING
310
WEINAN
2160
MT. HUASHAN
MUSEUM OF QIN
TERRACOTTA ARMY
AN
XI'AN
312
XIANGJISI
XINGJIAOSI
RWMAINS OF
LANTIAN-MAN
MT. NANWUTAI
210
Legend
Railway
Trunk highway
Nature reserve
County people's government
Village or town
Ancient monastery or temple
Ancient pagoda
Stone tablet
Ancient tomb
Site of historical interest

CHIEF EDITOR: WANG XIZHAO
ASSOCIATE EDITORS: YI XIONG, LI JIANHUA
EXECUTIVE EDITORS: GUO YOUMIN, WU XIAOCONG, LUO CHANG'AN
WRITERS: WU XIAOCONG, LUO CHANG'AN
PHOTOGRAPHER: GUO YOUMIN
TRANSLATOR: LING YUAN

图书在版编目(CIP)数据

世界历史名都西安/王锡钊编,—北京:中国旅游出版社,1996.7
ISBN 7-5032-1263-2
Ⅰ.世… Ⅱ王…Ⅲ.风光摄影—摄影集—中国—西安—英文 IV.J426.41
中国版本图书馆 CIP 数据核字(96)第 07513 号

XIAN: A FAMOUS ANCIENT CAPITAL IN THE WORLD
Edited by The Foreign Affairs Office Of Xian Municipal Government
Published by China Tourism Press
Platemade by Shenzhen Xingyu Printing & Platemaking Co., Ltd.
Printed by Shenzhen Sanwang Printing & Packing Co., Ltd.
First Edition, First Printing, August 1996
Large 16 Mo
5000 Copies
ISBN 7-5032-1263-2/K·206 (英文.平装)
0000100